'5 _

Lincoln on Trial

LINCOLN ON TRIAL

Southern
Civilians
and the
Law of War

Burrus M. Carnahan

THE UNIVERSITY PRESS OF KENTUCKY

Scholarly publisher for the Commonwealth,
serving Bellarmine University, Berea College, Centre College of Kentucky,
Eastern Kentucky University, The Filson Historical Society, Georgetown
College, Kentucky Historical Society, Kentucky State University, Morehead
State University, Murray State University, Northern Kentucky University,
Transylvania University, University of Kentucky, University of Louisville,
and Western Kentucky University.
All rights reserved.

Editorial and Sales Offices: The University Press of Kentucky
663 South Limestone Street, Lexington, Kentucky 40508-4008
www.kentuckypress.com

14 13 12 11 10   5 4 3 2 1

Library of Congress Cataloging-in-Publication Data

Carnahan, Burrus M., 1944–
  Lincoln on trial : southern civilians and the law of war / Burrus M.
Carnahan.
    p. cm.
  Includes bibliographical references and index.
  ISBN 978-0-8131-2569-5 (hardcover : alk. paper)
  1. Lincoln, Abraham, 1809–1865—Military leadership. 2. Lincoln,
Abraham, 1809–1865—Ethics. 3. United States—History—Civil War,
1861–1865—Moral and ethical aspects. 4. Civilians in war—Southern
States—History—19th century. 5. Combatants and noncombatants
(International law) 6. Just war doctrine. 7. War—Moral and ethical aspects
—United States—History—19th century. I. Title.
  E457.2.C295 2010
  973.7092—dc22   2009040204

This book is printed on acid-free recycled paper meeting
the requirements of the American National Standard
for Permanence in Paper for Printed Library Materials.

Manufactured in the United States of America.

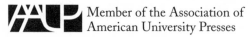 Member of the Association of
American University Presses

Actual war coming, blood grows hot, and blood is spilled. Thought is forced from old channels into confusion. Deception breeds and thrives. Confidence dies, and universal suspicion reigns. Each man feels an impulse to kill his neighbor, lest he be first killed by him. Revenge and retaliation follow. And all this, as before said, may be among honest men only. But this is not all. Every foul bird comes abroad, and every dirty reptile rises up. These add crime to confusion. Strong measures, deemed indispensable but harsh at best, such men make worse by mal-administration.

—Abraham Lincoln to Charles Drake and others,
October 5, 1863

Contents

Introduction

Crisis at Baltimore

Fort Sumter fell on April 14, 1861. Five days later, pro-Confederate mobs attacked Massachusetts infantry traveling through Baltimore en route to Washington, D.C., and the troops returned fire. To prevent further movement of U.S. troops through Baltimore, railroad bridges connecting that city to Washington and the North had been burned, not by saboteurs or guerrillas, but by organized members of the Maryland state militia acting with the approval of the mayor of Baltimore and the governor of the state. The Maryland legislature would soon assemble, perhaps to vote to secede and join the Confederacy, cutting the capital off from the rest of the United States.

On April 25, President Abraham Lincoln signed an order to General Winfield Scott, commander of the U.S. Army. If the Maryland legislature voted "to arm their people against the United States," Scott was "to adopt the most prompt, and efficient means to counteract, even, if necessary, to the bombardment of their cities."[1] The war was less than a month old, and already the president had authorized the army to turn artillery on American cities filled with unarmed men, women, and children. It was not a decision he made easily. His secretaries, John Nicolay and John Hay, recalled that the president's initial reaction was to seek conciliation. In the early morning of April 20, he assured a delegation from Baltimore that he would move future reinforcements around Baltimore, not through it. Attempting to lighten the situation with humor, Lincoln remarked: "If I grant you this, you shall come to-morrow demanding that no troops shall pass around."

The joke became a prophecy. Later that day one of Maryland's congressmen demanded that no U.S. troops travel through his state at all. The next day another delegation, led by the mayor of Baltimore, demanded that a body of Pennsylvania troops, who had reached a point fifteen miles north of Baltimore, be ordered to leave the state. "Fearing that renewed hostilities between soldiers and civilians might play into the hands of Maryland's secessionists," the president ordered the troops to return to Pennsylvania. Despite this order, Maryland militia destroyed the railroad bridges leading into the city, isolating Washington from the North. On April 22, another Baltimore delegation arrived in Washington to again ask that no troops pass through the state and added a demand that the president recognize the Confederacy. Lincoln had finally reached his limit, and he warned that if future reinforcements were attacked he would "lay Baltimore in ashes." Three days later he authorized the shelling of Baltimore if necessary to save Washington.[2]

Little in his background had prepared Abraham Lincoln to issue military orders endangering civilians. Nevertheless, he would grapple with similar issues repeatedly over the next four years. His most extreme critics would argue that, notwithstanding his humanitarian reputation, the president was at heart a bloody-minded autocrat, careless of innocent life and property. Jefferson Davis saw the Emancipation Proclamation as a deliberate attempt to incite the slaughter of white women and children, and Lord Richard Lyons, the British minister in Civil War Washington, appears to have agreed.[3] Even today, Lincoln's bitterest critics have not hesitated to charge him with waging a war of terror against unarmed civilians, to the extent of resorting to the inflammatory term "war crimes," a term unknown in the nineteenth century.[4]

Even if the most extreme of these charges are rejected as absurd, how are we to reconcile Lincoln the humanitarian, who hated the "monstrous injustice" of slavery, with Lincoln the relentless commander in chief, who would bombard the citizens of Baltimore to save the government in Washington? Answering this question will give us a new vantage point on the man himself, his personality, his philosophy, and his leadership.

A serious effort to analyze Lincoln's treatment of Southern civilians must start by determining what measures President Lincoln authorized, or at least which ones he knew about and did not oppose. Waging war against civilians is a very imprecise concept and could refer to a wide spectrum of activity. At its most serious, it would involve the deliberate killing of unarmed and unresisting civilian persons. At the other end of the scale would be the destruction or seizure of civilian property. Somewhere in between would lie restraints on personal liberty, such as arrest, exile, and forcible movement of civilians, and actions that, although not deliberately targeting civilians for destruction, increased the danger of injury to civilians. Among the latter would be destruction or seizure of crops and food, and the bombardment of fortified cities.

Determining what policies President Lincoln actually approved is important because Civil War armies on both sides were poorly disciplined and inflicted considerable hardship on civilians, both friendly and unfriendly, regardless of orders or official policy. One study of the impact of the war on civilians in Northern Virginia concluded that "hard war shocks obliterated much of Alexandria and Fairfax [counties] during the Civil War's first twelve months, a period that saw the two jurisdictions occupied by opposing, conventional armies whose top commanders espoused soft-war policies. Both consciously and unconsciously, their soldiers terrorized residents, devastated their property, and drove many from their homes."[5]

Active efforts to prevent harassment of civilians often proved futile. On the Union side, even General George B. McClellan, a stickler for respecting civilian property, could not prevent his troops from "accidentally" burning historic White House plantation (where George and Martha Washington were married) during the 1862 Peninsular Campaign.[6] Throughout the war, deserted houses tended to catch fire mysteriously whenever soldiers were around. In the summer of 1861, two frame houses belonging to Elcom G. Read in Fairfax County, Virginia, were burned down. One witness recounted that the fires were a simple act of vandalism: "They were burned by Union troops about two weeks after the first battle of Bull Run. I was standing near when they set fire to those buildings. The men belonged to the second Michigan [Volunteers] and were doing picket duty at the time. . . . I asked the soldiers why they did so and burn them buildings. They told me they were just making up a fire to roast some potatoes. I think they burned these buildings out of mischief."[7]

Abandoned houses that escaped arson were subject to another risk every fall, as both Union and Confederate armies went into winter quarters. Soldiers often dismantled houses, barns, and other sources of lumber to build winter huts, or "shebangs." After their house had been hit by eleven cannonballs during an 1861 skirmish at Dranesville, Virginia, Robert and Ann Coleman left the area for the duration of the war. Ann later told a U.S. claims commission that when they returned, they found no trace of the house: "No, not a particle of it. Not a piece of it. . . . Took the house all to pieces and built huts of it. The Union soldiers were in camp in Dranesville all that winter."[8]

During the Antietam campaign in September 1862, General Robert E. Lee wanted the people of Maryland to regard his soldiers not as invaders but rather as liberators from Lincoln's military tyranny, so he issued orders intended to minimize friction with the civilian population. Toward the end of the campaign, however, he confessed to President Jefferson Davis that these efforts had not been as successful as he had hoped:

> The presence of a large army in any country cannot but entail loss upon the inhabitants; it is necessary at times to remove fences, pass through fields on the march, and occupy them for encampments. In battles the destruction of property is also unavoidable and often very great; but, in addition to losses to individuals inseparable from a state of war, I regret to say that much unnecessary damage is done by the troops both while marching and in camp. It is impossible as the army is now organized to prevent these acts by orders. When such orders are published they are either imperfectly executed or wholly disregarded.[9]

With his subordinate commanders, Lee was more blunt: "The depredations committed by this army, its daily diminution by straggling, and the loss of arms thrown aside as too burdensome by stragglers, makes it necessary for preservation itself, aside from considerations of disgrace and injury to our cause arising from such outrages committed upon our citizens, that greater efforts be made by our officers to correct this growing evil."[10] Following the Antietam campaign, Lee's army withdrew to the Shenandoah Valley of Virginia, which had previously been occupied by an undisciplined Union force under the command of General Nathaniel Banks. As Lee's men "scoured the local countryside in search of provisions, taking anything and everything they could use," the generally pro-Confederate civilian population learned that it mattered little where their sympathies lay, since both armies seemed equally inclined to take or ruin their property.[11]

The problem never completely disappeared, even after General Lee's force had been reduced to a dedicated core of seasoned veterans. In late 1864, when the Army of Northern Virginia was defending the Confederate capital at the siege of Petersburg, General Lee still needed to condemn the mistreatment of local civilians: "The General Commanding has heard with pain and mortification that outrages and depredations amounting in some cases to flagrant robbery have been perpetrated upon citizens living within the lines, and near the camps of the army. Poor and helpless persons have been stripped of the means of subsistence and suffered violence by the hands of those upon whom they had a right to rely for protection. In one instance an atrocious murder was perpetrated upon a child by a band of ruffians whose supposed object was plunder."[12]

John Minor Botts, a prominent Virginia Unionist, also had an unfortunate opportunity to compare the behavior of the armies on both sides. In early 1864, he wrote to a friend:

> I had one of the finest farms in V[irgini]a and few persons anywhere were more comfortably fixed than I was, and I had hoped to spend the balance of my days here in comfort, and as I might have done, in luxury; but you can form no conception of the annoyances to which I have been subjected by the Confederate Army, and when the Federal Army came in, I had reason to hope for protection but so far from that, they have been equally destructive to my property as the other party, and the excuse they offer for it, is that I will be paid by the goverment for it all. . . . They have torn down and burnt my fencing in all directions, to the extent of many miles, taken away my gates, cut down my gate posts, and shade trees. . . . Out of 25 or 30 miles of fencing that I had this time last year, I haven't three left. . . . My timber is being so entirely destroyed, that I shall have none left, with which to enclose the farm again; and an estate worth all of $200,000 will by the time the Army leaves me, be nothing but a common or a waste.[13]

Botts ended with the philosophical observation that "the Officers generally are disposed to give me every protection, and so are the men, but there can be no Army without having in it many who are naturally vicious & destructive."

Not all Southern civilians found Union officers to be as sympathetic as those Botts encountered. Sometimes officers were just as vicious and destructive as the most depraved private soldier. In 1862, Colonel Carter Gazley of the 37th Indiana Volunteers was tried by court-martial and found guilty of stealing two horses from a civilian. Earlier that year, Colonel Charles A. de Villiers of the 31st Ohio Volunteers had been convicted by a court-martial of stealing $300 in currency and divers bonds and stock certificates from the safe of a lawyer in Point Pleasant, West Virginia.[14] Judge Thomas Morgan's house in Baton Rouge, Louisiana, was vandalized and looted by a pair of junior officers in August 1862. When one of the judge's daughters protested against the slashing of her father's portrait, one of the pair placed a pistol to her head and threatened to blow her brains out. The pillaging only stopped when an African American servant located a Federal officer willing to intervene:

> Charles caught a Captain Clark in the streets, when the work [of destruction] was almost over, and begged him to put an end to it. The gentleman went readily, but though the devastation was quite evident, no one was to be seen, and he was about to leave when, insisting that there was some one there, Charles drew him into [another daughter's] room, dived under the bed, and drew from thence a Yankee captain by one leg, followed by a lieutenant, each with a bundle of the boys' clothes which they instantly dropped, protesting they were only looking around the house. The gentleman captain carried them off to their superior.[15]

John Minor Botts had arrived at an important truth when he concluded that "there can be no Army without having in it many who are naturally vicious & destructive." Most crimes are committed by males in their late teens, twenties, and early thirties, the same demographic from which armies derive most of their soldiers.[16] Historically, armies in the field have always done significant damage to surrounding civilian communities with or without the sanction of their officers.

Of course, it would be equally wrong to absolve the Union army's command structure from any responsibility for rough treatment of civilian persons and property. Harsh measures were sometimes authorized, even, as in the case of the 1861 Baltimore riots, by the commander in chief. In assessing the legality and morality of such measures, the contemporary observer runs an unusually high risk of "presentism"—the error of judging the past by the moral and legal standards of the present day.

For example, the currently popular charge that Lincoln committed violations of the laws and customs of war implies that the president broke some rule of law that was actually in force during his term of office. Here the risk of presentism is especially high because the international standards of civilized warfare—the "laws and customs of war"—have changed radically since the time of Lincoln. The lengthy treaties and conventions reflecting these changes are written in legalistic, technical language, and even well-educated members of the public are often unaware of their significance.

Holding President Lincoln to anachronistic standards is not a practice limited to a fringe of Lincoln-haters and unreconstructed neo-Confederates. As recently as 1995, a highly distinguished professor of history wrote: "Had the Confederates somehow won, had their victory put them in position to bring their chief opponents before some sort of tribunal, they would have found themselves justified . . . in stringing up President Lincoln and the entire Union high command for violation of the laws of war, specifically for waging war against noncombatants."[17] In fact, as I discuss in the course of this book, the international standards of Lincoln's time often did not clearly distinguish between soldiers and noncombatant persons and property. More important, the concept of "command responsibility"—the legal theory that a military commander can sometimes be punished for failing to prevent war crimes committed by his subordinates—did not arise until after World War II.

Where treatment of enemy civilians is concerned, it is easy to make emotionally charged accusations against President Lincoln and his officers. Addressing such charges seriously is more difficult. As outlined above, that effort will require analysis of the numerous ways war could affect civilians, the sifting of data to determine what effects the president actually authorized, and, finally, an examination of the laws and customs of war as they then existed. This task is undertaken in the following chapters.

This study seeks an answer to the question, did President Lincoln authorize or condone violations of the laws of war, as they were understood in his time? The focus is on the words and actions of Abraham Lincoln in relation to enemy civilians. The study is not intended to present a comprehensive social, legal, or military history of the Civil War, nor is it a general biography of Lincoln. President Lincoln's policies are analyzed in order of their impact on Southern civilians, beginning, in chapter 2, with Lincoln's evolving policies on enemy private property, including the practice of "devastating" enemy territory. Chapter 3 then analyzes the president's attitude toward counter-guerrilla tactics of that era, which could include the execution of civilian hostages in retaliation for unlawful enemy actions. Lincoln's policy toward bombardment of cities is examined in chapter 4, and chapter 5 looks at his policy toward the deliberate killing of civilians, the hallmark of twentieth-century "total war."

President Lincoln probably authorized the bombardment of Baltimore at the urging of the army's general in chief, Winfield Scott. More typically, however, issues involving treatment of enemy civilians came to the president's attention through petitions from civilians affected by policies adopted by Union officers in the field. Deciding these appeals on a case by case basis, Lincoln developed general principles that could be applied to similar cases in the future. Lincoln's generals were, for example, frequently cautioned against engaging in acts of "revenge" motivated by hatred of the enemy. As a young man, Abraham Lincoln had responded to mob violence in Mississippi, Illinois, and Missouri by denouncing passion and revenge as the enemies of free government and calling on the people to apply "cold, calculating, unimpassioned reason" to defend the future of free political institutions.[18] As president, he was convinced that if military actions were to lead to a lasting peace, they must similarly be based on reason rather than emotion.

Curiously, although President Lincoln developed important general policies on the treatment of hostile civilian populations, he rarely used his powers as commander in chief to set out these policies in orders and proclamations for the guidance of his field commanders or members of his cabinet. On one occasion, his reluctance to publish his policies for the guidance of others led to a direct conflict with Secretary of War Edwin Stanton. The concluding chapter examines the general policies Lincoln adopted on enemy civilians, analyzes possible reasons for his reluctance to widely disseminate these policies, and suggests some insights these explorations may give us into Lincoln's character.

1

"With the Law of War in Time of War"

Applying International Law to a Civil War

At the beginning of the Civil War, Jefferson Davis and Abraham Lincoln had diametrically opposed views on the nature of the conflict and the laws that should apply to the conduct of hostilities and the treatment of enemy persons. The Confederate government argued that it represented an independent nation at war with another independent nation, and that their relations were regulated solely by international law. After secession, the Constitution of the United States was irrelevant, in the Confederate view.

In contrast, throughout the war Lincoln maintained that the Confederate states had not seceded, and could not secede, from the Union. In his view, the U.S. government was dealing not with a Confederate government, but with a group of rebellious individual citizens.[1] In principle, then, for Lincoln the Constitution, not international law, governed relations between the Federal government and its rebellious Southern citizens.

One result of this policy was that the Lincoln administration was extremely sensitive to any act that might accord a degree of legitimacy to the Confederate government, or to the rebellious state governments. The law of war applied to hostilities between independent nations, and applying it, in whole or in part, to the rebels could be another incremental step toward recognition of the Confederacy as a true government. Some of his Radical Republican critics believed President Lincoln had already stumbled in April 1861 when he declared a blockade of Southern ports, since under international law this effectively recognized the

9

rebels as "belligerents," allowing Britain, France, and other European powers to declare their neutrality in the conflict and maintain their trade with the Confederacy as a semi-sovereign entity.[2] The administration did not want to do anything that would inadvertently extend even more recognition to the Confederate States of America.

During the first year of the war, the president and his supporters clung to the belief that the majority of the Southern people were fundamentally loyal to the Union but had been misled by a small clique of secessionist politicians. If ordinary Southerners were handled with firmness and restraint, they believed, the "mystic chords of memory" binding all Americans together would eventually reassert their power and the insurrection would sputter out, as had the Whiskey Rebellion of 1794 and the South Carolina Nullification movement of 1833. Branding everyone in the South as public enemies of the U.S. government, subject to the law of war, would hardly advance this hoped-for process of early reconciliation.

The Federal government therefore faced an early dilemma in legal policy. Although there were good political reasons, at least at the start of the war, for the Lincoln administration to insist that the Constitution applied to its enemies, as the scope and intensity of the conflict grew the Confederate government used every means at its disposal to press Washington to apply the laws and customs of international war.

Between April and December 1861, the Lincoln administration and its military commanders in the field responded to these pressures by slowly applying more and more of the law of war to their dealings with the rebels. The process was gradual and unpublicized because of the administration's constant concern that according international rights to the Confederates would also grant them an increasing degree of international recognition. In the face of this dilemma, the Lincoln administration's initial reaction was to follow the course adopted by many other governments confronting hard choices—it tried to avoid taking a clear stand for as long as possible. Although the level of hostilities relentlessly grew in intensity throughout 1861, the Lincoln administration stubbornly refused to make a clear public choice between applying the law of war and applying peacetime Federal law to the rebels.

The administration's legal ambivalence at this early stage of the Civil War is illustrated by three issues faced by President Lincoln soon after the fall of Fort Sumter—the call for militia volunteers, the seizure of arms on the Mississippi River, and the declaration of a blockade. On April 15, 1861, immediately after Major Robert Anderson's surrender of Fort Sumter, the president issued a proclamation, citing the same statutory authority invoked by President Washington in the Whiskey Rebellion, calling 75,000 militia into Federal service. The declared purpose of this force was to "suppress" certain "combinations" of persons in the seceded states.

What is curious in retrospect is that, following the bombardment of a U.S. Army fort by heavy artillery manned by organized and uniformed military formations, the president did not declare these sinister combinations to be "levying War against" the United States, as treason is defined in the Constitution.[3] Rather, the president's proclamation described the Confederate army as "combinations too powerful to be suppressed by the ordinary course of judicial proceedings, or by the powers vested in the [U.S.] Marshals by law." Once these rebellious combinations had been suppressed, the president stated that the militia would "cause the laws to be duly executed" in the South. This is the language of peacetime law enforcement, not the waging of war. The reader is left with the impression that the 75,000 Federal soldiers would serve merely as an unusually large and colorfully dressed U.S. marshal's posse.[4]

The proclamation also declared that "the utmost care will be observed . . . to avoid any devastation, any destruction of, *or interference with, property*, or any disturbance of peaceful citizens in any part of the country."[5] Barely two weeks later, however, President Lincoln approved, or rather tried to approve, significant military interference with Southern property. This was an early hint that the White House knew that something more than a law enforcement approach might be needed to deal with the Confederacy and its armed forces.

On April 17, Governor Isham Harris of Tennessee refused the president's call for militia and telegraphed the secretary of war that "Tennessee will not furnish a single man for purpose of coercion, but 50,000, if necessary for the defense of our rights and those of our Southern brethren."[6] Thereafter, Governor Richard Yates of Illinois ordered his militia to seize a Mississippi riverboat, the *C. E. Hillman*, carrying munitions to pro-secession forces in Tennessee. On April 29, with an arrogant tone typical of "fire-eater" secessionists, Governor Harris wrote the president to protest that the Illinois government's "interruption of the free navigation of the Mississippi River and the seizure of property belonging to the State of Tennessee and her citizens" was "aggressive," "hostile," and an "outrage." He asked "by what authority the said acts were committed," and whether they were "done by or under the instructions of the Federal Government."[7]

Lincoln tried to draft a logical, lawyerly reply. While acknowledging that he had "no official information" about the incident, he nevertheless approved Governor Yates's action. Reminding Governor Harris that he had refused, "in disrespectful and malicious language," to provide Tennessee's quota of militia to the United States, the president concluded that the seizure logically followed from that refusal: "This Government therefore infers that munitions of War passing into the hands of said Governor, are intended to be used against the United States; and the government will not indulge the weakness of allowing it, so long as it is in it's power to prevent. This Government will not, at present, question, but that the State of Tennessee, by a majority of it's citizens, is loyal to the Federal Union, and the [U.S.] government holds itself responsible in damages for all injuries it may do to any who may prove to be such."[8] The president did not, however, tell Governor Harris what legal authority Governor Yates had to order the seizures. Indeed, he could not have done so without resolving the legal and political dilemma in which the administration found itself in April 1861.

Under the Constitution—the American law applicable between loyal citizens—the legality of the seizures was extremely doubtful. Governor Yates and the president had reasonable grounds for suspecting that these munitions would be used against the U.S. government, but that would not necessarily justify their seizure by the military without a warrant issued by a judge. In an 1851 opinion, *Mitchell v. Harmony*,[9] the Supreme Court had held a U.S. Army officer personally liable for the seizure and loss of a U.S. citizen's wagons and merchandise during the Mexican War, even though the officer and his superiors suspected that the property would fall into the hands of the Mexican government. Mr. Harmony was a New York merchant engaged in the overland trade between Missouri and the Mexican city of Santa Fe when war broke out between the United States and Mexico in 1846. After the capture of Santa Fe by U.S. forces, on December 14, 1846, a U.S. military expedition under the command of Colonel Alexander Doniphan set out from Santa Fe to invade northern Mexico. It was accompanied by a caravan of 300 merchants who hoped to reopen trade with southern Mexico that had been interrupted by the war.

Mr. Harmony joined this group in Santa Fe with his wagons and merchandise, but decided to leave the military column in January 1847 to strike out on his own, even though the expedition was then in the middle of enemy territory. Concerned that Harmony's wagons would be captured by Mexican forces, and foreseeing a military need to use them himself, Colonel Doniphan ordered Lieutenant Colonel David Mitchell to seize the wagons and mules. On February 28, Doniphan used the wagons as part of a mobile fortification in a battle for the city of Chihuahua. Having seen hard service in the war, Harmony's broken down wagons were abandoned by the army when it withdrew from Chihuahua on April 23, 1847.[10]

After the war, Harmony sued Mitchell for the value of his wagons, mules, and merchandise, and the case eventually came before the U.S. Supreme Court. It might be thought that a merchant who voluntarily joined a military force invading enemy territory would assume the risk that he would not be allowed to leave the column without the commanding officer's permission, and that his property might be damaged during combat with the enemy. Whatever the merchant's reasonable expectations in this situation, it might be thought that an army officer, acting in his official capacity in enemy territory to prevent the wagons from leaving, would not be held personally liable for damage to the merchant's property.

Chief Justice Roger Taney, speaking for the Court, would have none of this. Harmony was a U.S. citizen, and under the Fifth Amendment to the Constitution private property could not be taken for public use without just compensation. The army had no legal right to order Lieutenant Colonel Mitchell to seize Harmony's goods, so Mitchell could not use superior orders as a defense. The Supreme Court upheld a judgment against Mitchell for more than $90,000 in damages, plus $5,000 in court costs.

The furthest Chief Justice Taney would go to acknowledge that military considerations might have some impact on the property rights of citizens was to concede that private property might be taken for public service, or to prevent it from falling into enemy hands, where "the danger is immediate, and impending; or the necessity urgent for the public service, such as will not admit of delay." In such a case, the officer would not be personally liable, but still "the government is bound to make full compensation to the owner."[11] Taney was still chief justice in 1861, and the Illinois officers who seized the *C. E. Hillman* and its cargo risked being held liable to the ship's owners and the state of Tennessee, if Governor Harris and his supporters were still considered loyal American citizens.

Only under the laws of war, using their respective powers as commanders in chief of the Illinois militia and the U.S. Army, could Governor Yates and President Lincoln have justified the seizure of another state's munitions and a privately owned river boat. But invoking the law of war would have expressly labeled Governor Harris and his forces as enemies, rebels with whom the United States was at war. This would have directly contradicted the president's statement that he was not questioning the loyalty of Tennessee or its citizens. At this stage, the Lincoln administration was desperately trying to hold in the Union as many border slave states as possible. Labeling Governor Harris and his supporters as enemies might be just the act that would push Tennessee into open secession. In fact, Tennessee seceded on June 8, 1861, and Governor Harris later fled south before advancing Union armies.

Nevertheless, the draft letter reflects President Lincoln's early determination not to allow peacetime property law to impede the suppression of the rebellion, even if he could not, as yet, publicly identify a legal foundation for this decision. The armies of the Union would respect private property to the extent they could, but when there was a clear conflict between property rights and military effectiveness, the president had already made his choice.

To a limited extent, the Lincoln administration had already been forced to apply the international law of war to its dealings with the rebels. On April 19, the president declared a blockade of the ports in the Confederate states, pursuant to "the laws of the United States and the law of Nations, in such case provided."[12] The term "blockade" carried a definite burden of meaning in international law, and its use meant the United States was claiming clearly defined rights under international law, and recognizing corresponding obligations, in relations with Britain, France, and other neutral nations.

Declaring a blockade also meant, however, that the United States was acknowledging that the Confederates were "belligerents," that is, that they had at least a limited international status, short of recognition as an independent nation, so long as the war continued. This had the effect of according neutral governments both the right and the obligation to deal even-handedly with the United States and the Confederate States, giving military assistance to neither side. Under the international law of the time, "belligerency" was an intermediate status between the total sovereignty of an independent nation and a mere insurgency, which gave a rebel group no international status at all. To be legally entitled to recognition as a belligerent power, a rebel movement had to meet certain tests—it had to have an organized government that controlled a certain territory of its own, and its armed forces had themselves to comply with the international laws of war.[13] By declaring a blockade of the Confederate coast, and demanding that neutral nations respect that blockade, the Lincoln administration was in effect recognizing that the rebels were a belligerent power. Neutral countries could accord the Confederacy, as a belligerent power, all the rights and privileges of a sovereign nation at war, so long as the conflict lasted, such as allowing Confederate warships to use a neutral's seaports.

As a practical matter, recognition of belligerency for a rebel group was often only a step toward recognizing the independence of a new nation. For that reason, the Lincoln administration naturally shied away from accepting the full implications of its blockade declaration. When England and France accepted that the Confederacy was a belligerent power by issuing declarations of neutrality, the reaction of the Lincoln administration was hostile.

To avoid recognizing the Confederates as belligerents, the administration had considered the alternative of ordering the closure to international commerce of all ports in the seceded states. Every nation has the sovereign right to establish commercial ports of entry into its territory and to close those ports at will. Since the Federal government viewed secession as illegal and without effect, commerce with Confederate ports was, so the argument ran, still under the sovereign control of the United States. In other words, the administration would have preferred closing Southern ports by using internal U.S. customs laws, not the international law of war.[14]

The problem with this course of action was that whatever the policy was called, as a practical matter it would have to be enforced by U.S. Navy warships operating in international waters (the "high seas") outside the three-mile territorial limit claimed by the United States. Under international law, on the high seas warships enforcing a blockade had the right to stop and search merchant vessels from neutral nations, and even to seize those that had already violated the blockade or had cargo destined for a blockaded port. No similar rights were recognized to enforce a nation's closure of its own ports. If a warship stopped another country's merchant ships on the high seas to determine whether they were going to or coming from a closed port, it would be violating the internationally recognized freedom of the seas. If the United States tried to implement the closure of Southern ports by forcibly stopping and inspecting British and French shipping on the high seas, those countries would almost certainly go to war to defend their rights. Like it or not, then, the closure of Confederate ports had to be accomplished through a blockade—that is, by applying the international law of war to seaports under Confederate control.

Reflecting the reluctance of the Lincoln administration to accord any legitimacy to the Confederate government, another part of the blockade proclamation rejected international law as the basis for other relations with rebel forces. In its preamble, the proclamation noted that the Confederate government (referred to as "a combination of persons, engaged in . . . insurrection") had "threatened to grant pretended letters of marque to authorize the bearers thereof to commit assaults on the lives, vessels, and property of good citizens of the country lawfully engaged in commerce on the high seas and in waters of the United States." Under nineteenth-century international law, a letter of marque was a government license authorizing a privately owned warship, referred to as a "privateer," to prey on enemy merchant vessels, or even on neutral vessels carrying military supplies ("contraband") to the enemy.

Captured merchant ships were to be brought before the courts of the government that had issued the letter of marque for a determination as to whether the capture was proper under international law. The issues before a prize court might include, for example, whether the cargo of a neutral vessel was truly contraband (legal opinions varied widely on the proper definition), or whether a ship flying a neutral flag was in fact an enemy merchant ship carrying false papers (sham transactions "transferring" a ship to a neutral owner were common). If the courts approved the capture, the ship was said to be "condemned as a prize" and sold. The proceeds of sale were divided between the government, the owners of the privateer, and its crew according to a formula set by the government issuing the letter of marque. In effect, privateering was a legalized form of piracy. Profit was the motive for privateers.[15]

The Confederate government had announced that it would issue letters of marque for privateers to prey on Union merchant shipping.[16] Since the Lincoln administration did not recognize the legitimacy of the Confederate government, it was determined not to recognize the legality of any privateering under Confederate authority. In its April 19 blockade proclamation, the Lincoln administration announced that it would refuse to recognize the legitimacy of letters of marque issued by the Confederate government. If any Confederate privateers were captured by U.S. forces, the crew members would be treated as criminals, not prisoners of war: "And I hereby proclaim and declare that if any person under the pretended authority of the said States, or under any other pretense, shall molest a vessel of the United States, or the persons or cargo on board of her, such persons will be held amenable to the laws of the United States for the prevention and punishment of piracy."

As a logical matter, the declared intention to treat Confederate privateers as pirates was difficult to reconcile with the decision to impose a blockade on Confederate ports. A blockade would be legitimate, and entitled to respect from other nations, only if it had been imposed as a military measure during a war between nations, or in a civil war between a government and an insurgent group recognized as a belligerent power. However, if the Confederacy was a belligerent, then under the law of war it had the power to exercise belligerent rights, to include issuing letters of marque.

Thus, President Lincoln's April 19, 1861, blockade proclamation both claimed rights against the Confederates under the international law of war and declared that he would refuse to recognize the rights of Confederate sailors under the same body of law. Along with the April 15 proclamation calling up the militia and the May draft response to the governor of Tennessee, the blockade proclamation illustrates the ambiguous, and even confused, early policy of the Lincoln administration on the law governing its suppression of the rebellion.

By the summer of 1861, however, the Lincoln administration had come to accept that the Civil War had reached such a scale of violence that as a practical matter it would have to grant Confederate forces at least some rights under the international law of war. On July 12, Army Quartermaster General Montgomery Meigs advised Secretary of War Simon Cameron, perhaps at the secretary's request, that the army should start to plan for the reception and treatment of prisoners of war, noting that under the law of war "prisoners of war are entitled to proper accommodations, to courteous and respectful treatment, to one ration a day and to consideration according to rank."[17]

Things came to a head when U.S. forces in Ohio, under the command of General George B. McClellan, invaded the northwestern counties of Virginia. The inhabitants of this region were generally pro-

Union, and later formed the new state of West Virginia. On July 13, Lieutenant Colonel John Pegram of the Confederate army surrendered himself and more than 500 of his men to McClellan's forces. McClellan telegraphed army headquarters that as a condition of surrender he had agreed "to treat them with the kindness due prisoners of war, but stating that it was not in my power to relieve them from any liability incurred by taking arms against the United States." When Pegram's men were added to prisoners already taken, McClellan would have almost 1,000 Confederate soldiers in his custody. He asked the War Department for "immediate instructions by telegraph as to the disposition to be made of officers and men taken [as] prisoners."[18] On July 14, General Winfield Scott, commanding general of the army, wired McClellan that the surrendered Confederate soldiers were to be regarded as prisoners of war.[19] This precedent would thereafter be followed throughout the Civil War.

Communicating with the enemy under a flag of truce was an old custom under the laws of war. From the very beginning of the conflict, Federal officers in the field had communicated with their Confederate counterparts under flags of truce, ostensibly without the knowledge or authorization of their superiors in the national capital. By the end of July 1861, the passage of a flag-of-truce boat between the generals commanding Fortress Monroe and the Confederate port of Norfolk, Virginia, had become routine.

The need for quasi-official communications under a flag of truce seems to have been reluctantly accepted by the Lincoln administration in mid-August 1861. As of August 2, Secretary of State William H. Seward had no official channel to ask the Confederate authorities whether Congressman Alfred Ely of New York had been killed or taken prisoner at Bull Run; instead, he relied on a private telegram to confirm the congressman's capture. On August 22, however, Secretary of War Cameron did not hesitate to direct that twenty-three paroled Confederate prisoners be returned to the South on the flag-of-truce boat running between Norfolk and Fortress Monroe.[20]

The decision to seek formal negotiation of a prisoner exchange cartel, in accordance with the laws of war, was the most difficult for the Lincoln administration to accept. In principle, military-to-military agreements for solely military purposes had no political implications under international law. Under the laws of war, field commanders could, for example, agree to a truce or cease-fire to remove the wounded from a battlefield, to exchange prisoners of war, or to negotiate terms of surrender for an army facing defeat, without recognizing the legitimacy of the enemy's government. The wars of the twentieth century have provided many examples of this principle. Cease-fires were negotiated between Arab and Israeli field commanders in 1948, 1956, and 1967, without compromising the refusal of Arab governments to recognize the state of Israel. The Korean War was ended by a military-to-military cease-fire in 1953 that allowed both sides to avoid recognizing the legitimacy of the Korean government on the other side.

Nevertheless, flags of truce could be exchanged, and military-to-military agreements entered into, only with enemy belligerents in a war, and not with pirates, bandits, or criminal organizations of traitors. As late as December 10, 1861, Attorney General Edward Bates objected in a cabinet meeting to regular prisoner exchanges because he believed they granted too much legitimacy to the Confederacy.[21] Bates's concerns were shared by politically sensitive Union officers in the field. In October, Ulysses S. Grant, then an obscure general in the Western theater of war, informed Confederate general Leonidas Polk that "in regard to the exchange of prisoners proposed I can of my own accord make none. I recognize no Southern Confederacy myself but will communicate with higher authority for their views."[22] Another Federal general replied to a similar request in more detail: "I am in receipt of your communication dated on the 24th instant requesting an exchange of prisoners. To do this would imply that the Government of the United States admits the existing civil war to be between independent nations. This I cannot admit and must therefore decline to make any terms or conditions in reference to those we mutually hold as prisoners taken in arms without the orders of my Government."[23] Tortuous subterfuges were adopted to avoid the appearance of negotiating with the rebels. A paroled Confederate prisoner might be sent back through his own lines to arrange the release of a Union prisoner of equal rank, after which he would be formally released from the terms of his parole.[24] Another common fiction was to arrange for parallel "humanitarian" releases of a certain number of prisoners by each side.[25]

It was, of course, in the Confederacy's interest to avoid subterfuge and insist on formal prisoner exchanges, and to institutionalize the exchanges in a formal agreement, or "exchange cartel," between the two sides. Uncertainty over the fate of Union prisoners taken at Bull Run and later Confederate victories led to increased pressure for exchanges from the North as well as the South. Relatives of soldiers held by the Confederates urged the government to do something to secure the release of their loved ones. In turn, congressmen, loyal state governors, and influential private citizens urged Lincoln to negotiate an exchange of prisoners.[26] On December 11, 1861, the House of Representatives passed a resolution requesting the president "to inaugurate systematic measures for the exchange of prisoners in the present rebellion."[27]

In January 1862, the Confederate authorities tried to initiate negotiations for a formal prisoner exchange cartel through the channel of communications between Norfolk and Fortress Monroe. In early February, the Lincoln administration capitulated on this issue in response to domestic and Confederate pressure. On January 20, Confederate general Benjamin Huger, commanding the garrison at Norfolk, wrote to his Union counterpart that the Confederate government was "willing and anxious to exchange prisoners on fair terms, and as the authorities at Washington have permitted it in certain cases I beg your assistance in making it general and thus aid the cause of humanity and civilization."[28] Noting that the letter was "worthy of consideration," General John Wool forwarded it to army headquarters: "As the exchange of prisoners is now established would it not save you and myself a great deal of labor and trouble if the two Governments appointed agents to attend to it? It could be done with more system and regularity, and the officers and men might be kept together."[29]

On February 11, Edwin M. Stanton, the new secretary of war, directed the commanding general at Fortress Monroe to begin cartel negotiations with his counterpart at Norfolk:

> You will inform General Huger that you alone are clothed with full powers for the purpose of arranging for exchange of prisoners. . . . You may arrange for the restoration of all the prisoners to their homes on fair terms of exchange, man for man and officer for officer of equal grade, assimilating the grade of officers of the Army and Navy when necessary, and agreeing upon equitable terms for the number of men of officers of inferior grade to be exchanged for any of higher grade when the occasion shall arise. That all the surplus prisoners on either side to be discharged on parole, with the agreement that any prisoners of war taken by the other party shall be returned in exchange as fast as captured, and this system to be continued while hostili-

ties continue so that on all occasions either party shall so hold them only on parole till exchanged, the prisoners being allowed to remain in their own region till the exchange is effected.[30]

The initial negotiations did not go well. On February 23, representatives of the two sides met and exchanged drafts for an exchange cartel. The Confederate draft agreement included a provision that the capturing party would transport paroled or exchanged prisoners to the "frontier of their own country free of expense to the prisoners and at the expense of the capturing party." This phrase was politically loaded, since it implied that the United States and the Confederacy were two different countries. General Wool sensed that there was something wrong with this provision from the Union point of view, but couldn't quite put his finger on it. He therefore objected to it for reasons of cost and requested further instructions from Washington.[31] The secretary of war saw the proposal as evidence of Confederate bad faith and told Wool to break off negotiations: "The proposition is obnoxious in its terms and import and wholly inadmissible, and as the terms you were authorized to offer have not been accepted you will make no arrangement at present except for actual exchanges."[32] Confederate commissioner Howell Cobb then offered to change the language to provide for return of prisoners to the "frontier of the line of hostilities," a politically neutral phrase.[33] By then, so much suspicion had been aroused on the Union side that the negotiations dragged on for months, and an exchange cartel was not signed until July 22, 1862. Just by entering into these negotiations, however, the Lincoln administration was conceding that Confederate soldiers and sailors would be prisoners of war, treated in accordance with the international laws of war, at least as long as the conflict continued.

While the Union's decision to apply the laws of war was beneficial to captured Confederate soldiers and sailors, it would have a very different effect on the treatment of Confederate civilians. If Confederate fighting men were to be accorded the privileges of lawful combatants under the laws of war, then it was only logical that secessionist civilians should suffer the disadvantages that the law of war imposed on enemy citizens in wartime. Hostile civilians would be treated not as U.S. citizens but as enemy aliens who had no rights under the U.S. Constitution or the Bill of Rights. Under international law, the freedom of enemy citizens could be sharply curtailed and their property was subject to seizure or destruction. Two nineteenth-century decisions of the U.S.

Supreme Court illustrate the importance of the distinction between enemy civilians and U.S. citizens.

The first case, *United States v. Brown*, arose out of the War of 1812 with England.[34] Just before the war, several London merchants had hired the American ship *Emulous* to take 550 tons of pine lumber from Savannah, Georgia, to Plymouth, England. On April 18, 1812, the *Emulous* sailed from Savannah to her home port at New Bedford, Massachusetts, where the lumber was unloaded while the ship underwent repairs. Thereafter, Congress declared war on Great Britain, and the owner of the *Emulous*, John Delano, seized the lumber and informed the U.S. district attorney for Massachusetts that enemy property was present in his district. The U.S. attorney filed suit on behalf of the United States and Delano, asking the court to declare the lumber forfeited to the United States as enemy property. (As an "informer," Delano could claim part of the value of the condemned lumber as a reward for having informed the U.S. authorities of the location of enemy alien property.) Armitz Brown purchased the British merchants' rights in the lumber and defended his right to it, arguing that the most modern authorities on the law of war opposed confiscating the property of enemy nationals that happened to be in a country's territory at the time its government declared war.

At that time, Supreme Court justices presided over lower Federal courts when the higher tribunal was not in session. At the trial of this case, Joseph Story upheld the seizure of the pine logs as a legitimate war measure. By declaring war on Great Britain, he reasoned, Congress had given the president all the powers necessary to win the war. These powers were defined by the law of nations, which allowed any government at war to confiscate the private property of enemy citizens.

Brown appealed Story's decision to the Supreme Court. There, Chief Justice John Marshall made it clear that he and the other justices agreed with Justice Story that the law of war allowed the seizure and forfeiture of any private property owned by persons living under the control of the enemy government: "Respecting the power of government, no doubt is entertained. *That war gives to the sovereign full right to take the persons and confiscate the property of the enemy, wherever found, is conceded.* The mitigations of this rigid rule, which the humane and wise policy of modern times has introduced into practice, will more or less affect the exercise of this right, but cannot impair the right itself."[35]

In the end, Mr. Brown, representing the interests of the British property owners, won the suit. Without denying the sovereign power of the United States to confiscate the property of alien enemies, Chief Justice Marshall nevertheless concluded that under the constitutional scheme of the United States, only Congress could authorize the seizure and forfeiture of enemy private property, at least the seizure of property found in American territory at the commencement of hostilities. No statute authorizing such forfeiture had been passed; indeed, the only statute dealing in any way with enemy alien property seemed to lean in favor of the owners of the pine logs. (Not surprisingly, Justice Story dissented from the Court's decision to reverse his lower court opinion.)

At the time of the Civil War, the *Brown* decision was still the leading American legal precedent on treatment of enemy private property under the laws of war. Thus, under the laws of war, the U.S. government and its military arms were not required to respect any rights of the owner of private property belonging to an enemy national. Conversely, under the *Mitchell v. Harmony* precedent, private property owned by an American citizen must be fully respected, even in wartime.[36] At the start of the Civil War, however, it was not clear which legal precedent should apply to the citizens of seceded states. The official position of the Lincoln administration was that acts of secession were void and that citizens of seceded states were still U.S. citizens. Nevertheless, the laws of war were being applied to the Confederate armies, and large-scale military operations would be impossible if every affected civilian was accorded full rights under the Constitution.

Fortunately for the Lincoln government, the opinions of Chief Justice Marshall and Justice Story in the *Brown* case provided a way out of the dilemma. Both of these leading jurists agreed that under the Constitution, the war powers of the Federal government authorized the United States to take any action authorized by the international laws of war. By their reasoning, it must be assumed that the Founders, when they granted Congress and the president the power to make war, wanted the United States to win its wars. Therefore, the Constitution must also have granted the Federal government all the legitimate powers any potential enemy nation would have had—"all the ordinary rights of belligerents." What those war-winning rights were could be determined by looking at the crystallized experiences and practices of other warmaking governments—the laws and customs of war.

Justice Story extended this reasoning to the war powers of the president. He argued that as commander in chief of the army and navy, the president "must, as an incident of the office, have a right to employ all the usual and customary means acknowledged in war, to carry it [i.e., a declaration of war] into effect."[37] Furthermore, this "power to carry war into effect gives every incidental power which the law of nations authorizes and approves in a state of war."[38] By the twentieth century, Story's theory that the president's war powers extend to any measure authorized by international law had become generally accepted by the courts and legal scholars.[39]

This was all very well for an international war declared by Congress, but it left open the question of whether the president had the belligerent rights granted by the law of war when engaged in fighting an internal rebellion. Fortunately, in 1849 the U.S. Supreme Court had addressed the issue of executive power to suppress rebels in the context of a rebellion against state authority. The case of *Luther v. Borden* arose from a minor insurrection in Rhode Island over proposals to reform the state constitution, which had not been changed since the Revolutionary War. In response, the governor called out the state militia and declared martial law. After things settled down, several persons who had been detained and whose houses had been searched by the militia sued the military officers involved. In an opinion by Chief Justice Taney, the U.S. Supreme Court ruled firmly in favor of the state government:

> Unquestionably a State may use its military power to put down an armed insurrection too strong to be controlled by the civil authority. The power is essential to the existence of every government, essential to the preservation of order and free institutions, and is as necessary to the States of this Union as to any other government. The State itself must determine what degree of force the crisis demands. And if the government of Rhode Island deemed the armed opposition so formidable and so ramified throughout the State as to require the use of its military force and the declaration of martial law, we see no ground upon which this court can question its authority. *It was a state of war, and the established government resorted to the rights and usages of war to maintain itself, and to overcome the unlawful opposition.*[40]

This 1849 decision established the principle that to suppress an internal rebellion a state governor could take forceful measures against his state's rebellious citizens, so long as those measures were authorized by the international law of war. By analogy, the president of the United

States should have the power to use similar measures against U.S. citizens when repressing a rebellion against the United States, particularly when the rebels themselves have been accorded belligerent rights under "the rights and usages of war." In contrast, the 1851 decision in *Mitchell v. Harmony* established that, even in time of war, the executive branch had to respect constitutional rights of U.S. citizens who were not supporting the enemy.[41]

Which of these two precedents would apply to the president's powers to wage the Civil War? This question came before the Supreme Court as a result of the blockade of Confederate ports declared by President Lincoln in April 1861. Three ships owned by American citizens were captured by the U.S. Navy and brought into court to be condemned as prizes of war. The owners argued that declaring a blockade was beyond the president's powers as commander in chief of the navy, particularly in a civil war that had not been declared by Congress. In 1863, by a five-to-four vote, the Court held that the president had the same war powers in the Civil War as he would in an international conflict, and that the blockade runners were lawful prizes under the law of war:

As a civil war is never publicly proclaimed . . . against insurgents, its actual existence is a fact in our domestic history which the Court is bound to notice and to know.

The true test of its existence, as found in the writings of the sages of the common law, may be thus summarily stated: "When the regular course of justice is interrupted by revolt, rebellion, or insurrection, so that the Courts of Justice cannot be kept open, civil war exists and hostilities may be prosecuted on the same footing as if those opposing the Government were foreign enemies invading the land." . . .

Whether the President in fulfilling his duties, as Commander-in-Chief, in suppressing an insurrection, has met with such armed hostile resistance, and a civil war of such alarming proportions as will compel him to accord to them the character of belligerents, is a question to be decided by him, and this Court must be governed by the decisions and acts of the political department of the Government to which this power was entrusted. "He must determine what degree of force the crisis demands." The proclamation of blockade is itself official and conclusive evidence to the Court that a state of war existed which demanded and authorized a recourse to such a measure, under the circumstances peculiar to the case. . . .

We are of the opinion that the President had a right, *jure belli* [by the law of war], to institute a blockade of ports in possession of the States in rebellion, which neutrals are bound to regard.[42]

The dissenting opinion, written by Justice Samuel Nelson, conceded that the federal government could, in principle, use all powers granted by the law of nations to suppress a rebellion. However, unlike the majority, who regarded the question of whether a war existed as an issue of fact that the president could determine, the dissenters believed that only Congress could recognize the existence of a civil war:

In the case of a rebellion or resistance of a portion of the people of a country against the established government, there is no doubt, if in its progress and enlargement the government thus sought to be overthrown sees fit, it may by the competent power recognize or declare the existence of a state of civil war, which will draw after it all the consequences and rights of war between the contending parties as in the case of a public [international] war. . . .

But before this insurrection against the established Government can be dealt with on the footing of a civil war, within the meaning of the law of nations and the Constitution of the United States, and which will draw after it belligerent rights, it must be recognized or declared by the war-making power of the Government. . . .

Congress alone can determine whether war exists or should be declared, and until they have acted, no citizen of the State can be punished in his person or property unless he has committed some offence against a law of Congress passed before the act was committed which made it a crime and defined the punishment. The penalty of confiscation for the acts of others with which he had no concern cannot lawfully be inflicted.[43]

In reply, the Court majority noted that Congress had, in fact, approved the president's actions, including the proclamation of blockade, retroactively:

If it were necessary to the technical existence of a war that it should have a legislative sanction, we find it in almost every act passed at the extraordinary session of the Legislature of 1861, which was wholly employed in enacting laws to enable the Government to prosecute the war with vigor and efficiency. And finally, in 1861, we find Congress . . . in anticipation of such astute objections [as in the dissent], passing an act "approving, legalizing, and making valid all the acts, proclamations, and orders of the President, &c., as if they had been *issued and done under the previous express authority* and direction of the Congress of the United States."[44]

Chief Justice Taney was among the four dissenters. He did not write a dissent of his own and instead joined in Justice Nelson's opinion, so we do not know how or whether he was able to reconcile in his own mind Nelson's dissent and his own 1849 opinion in *Luther v. Borden*. The answer may lie in an unpublished memorandum found among Taney's papers in which he concluded that the United States could not legally use military force to prevent a state from seceding from the Union.[45] Whatever his reasoning might have been, the chief justice who administered the oath of office to Abraham Lincoln could not bring himself to grant the president of the United States the same war powers he had willingly accorded the governor of Rhode Island.

Later in 1863, President Lincoln explained his own views of presidential power under law of war when defending the legality of the Emancipation Proclamation in a public letter to James C. Conkling:

You dislike the emancipation proclamation; and, perhaps would have it retracted. You say it is unconstitutional—I think differently. I think the constitution invests its commander-in-chief, with the law of war in time of war—The most that can be said, if so much, is that slaves are property. Is there—has there ever been—any question that by the law of war, property, both of enemies and friends, may be taken when needed? And is it not needed whenever taking it, helps us, or hurts the enemy? Armies, the world over, destroy enemies' property when they can not use it; and even destroy their own to keep it from the enemy. Civilized belligerents do all in their power to help themselves, or hurt the enemy, except a few things regarded as barbarous or cruel. Among the exceptions are the massacres of vanquished foes, and non-combatants, male and female.[46]

Applying the laws and customs of war to Confederate soldiers and civilians created a unique challenge for the Union high command. When the Civil War started, there were only 16,000 men in the regular army. By 1865, 2,200,000 men were still under arms or had served in the Union army.[47] To lead this mass army, large numbers of civilians were commissioned as officers of volunteers, almost all of whom were unacquainted with the international laws and customs of war.

Even many regular army officers were poorly equipped to instruct their amateur brother officers in this arcane branch of legal study. During the War with Mexico, Winfield Scott, the army's general in chief, could provide valuable guidance to his subordinates based on his legal studies as a young man and his thorough mastery of European military history and practice, but little effort was made to preserve this experience before he retired in the fall of 1861. In the 1850s, a board of officers convened by the War Department had recommended that Congress enact a statute defining the civil powers of army officers who were required to govern occupied enemy territory, but Congress had ignored the recommendation. General Scott had also proposed that Dr. Francis Lieber of Columbia College (now Columbia University) teach a course on the law of war at West Point, but this idea had also been dropped when the academy superintendent objected that the curriculum was already overcrowded.[48]

One officer who was well equipped with knowledge of the laws of war was Major General Henry Halleck. An 1831 graduate of West Point (third in a class of thirty-one cadets), Halleck left the army in 1854 to practice law in San Francisco. He wrote several books on legal and military subjects, including a respected multivolume treatise on international law. At the start of the Civil War, he returned to the army and was promoted to major general.

At the end of 1861, Halleck was appointed to command the Department of the Missouri, where he found that much of Missouri had descended to near anarchy. Sabotage, pillage, and guerrilla warfare were rife, while bands of paramilitary marauders, with only the most tenuous connection to either the U.S. or Confederate governments, preyed on the civilian population. These acts were violations of the laws of war, but General Halleck found that the regular and volunteer officers under his command were unfamiliar with this body of law and the procedures for enforcing it. General John Pope, for example, had ordered captured guerrillas to be tried by military commissions, even though he lacked the legal authority to convene such courts.[49]

At the end of August 1861, one of Halleck's predecessors, General John Frémont, had added to the confusion when he issued a poorly worded proclamation declaring that all "persons who shall be taken with arms in their hands within [Union] lines shall be tried by court-martial and if found guilty will be shot." In addition, all "property of those who shall take up arms against the United States or who shall be directly proven to have taken an active part with their enemies in the field" was declared confiscated and any slaves they held were "hereby declared free men."[50] This premature emancipation proclamation caused a furor in the neighboring slave state of Kentucky, which had not yet decided whether to secede. To save Kentucky for the Union, President Lincoln requested, and eventually ordered, that this part of Frémont's proclamation be modified to conform to the existing acts of Congress on forfeiture of rebel property.

The sentence requiring those "taken with arms in their hands within [Union] lines" to be shot caused its own problems. One of Frémont's subordinates even asked whether he should shoot wounded Confederate soldiers left on the field of battle. Horrified, Frémont replied that he wanted it "clearly understood that the proclamation is intended distinctly to recognize all the usual rights of an open enemy in the field and to be in all respects strictly conformable to the ordinary usages of war."[51] President Lincoln also modified the order to require that all death sentences be reviewed at the White House.

Although Halleck was a mediocre general, he was a very good lawyer, and in early 1862 he set about clearing up the legal mess left by his predecessors in command. On January 1, 1862, General Halleck published a general order for his department that laid out basic concepts of the laws of war as well as the proper procedures for their enforcement through trials before military commissions. In particular, he clarified the distinction between hostilities carried out by members of the regular Confederate forces in open combat and unlawful actions by both regular forces and unauthorized guerrilla bands. A soldier "duly enrolled and authorized to act in a military capacity in the enemy's service" was not to be punished "for the taking of human life in battle, siege, &c.," but could be punished for acts committed in violation of the laws of war.

"Thus he cannot be punished by a military tribunal for committing acts of hostility which are authorized by the laws of war but if he has committed murder, robbery, theft, arson, &c. the fact of his being a prisoner of war does not exempt him from trial by a military tribunal." However, "insurgents not militarily organized under the laws of the State, predatory partisans and guerrilla bands" were "in a legal sense mere freebooters and banditti" and were "liable to the same punishment which was imposed upon guerrilla bands by Napoleon in Spain, and by Scott in Mexico."[52] Napoleon and Scott had punished guerrillas with death.

Military commissions were, according to Halleck's order, the proper tribunals to punish freebooters, banditti, and guerrillas. Military commissions had to be composed of a minimum of three officers and could be convened only by orders from the commanding general of the U.S. Army or a military department. Sentences could not be carried out until they had been approved by the convening officer. When he took command of the entire U.S. Army in the summer of 1862, Halleck saw the need for similar but more extensive guidance to be available for all officers of the army, and he asked Dr. Francis Lieber to advise a board of officers who would draw up a more complete codification of the laws and customs of war. In the end, Lieber did all the writing, and the document, issued by the War Department as General Order 100 on April 24, 1863, has since been known as the Lieber Code.[53]

Born in Prussia in 1798, Francis Lieber served as a soldier in the final campaign of the Napoleonic Wars in 1815, and in 1820 he participated in the Greek war for independence. While a professor at the University of Jena, he was persecuted by the Prussian government for his democratic political opinions and fled to England. In 1827, he immigrated to America. Although he was strongly antislavery, Lieber denied being an abolitionist. He was familiar with the culture of the South, having taught at South Carolina College for several years before coming to Columbia College in New York. For Francis Lieber, the law of war was more than an academic subject, since his own family was divided by the Civil War. Two of his sons served in the Union army and one was killed fighting for the Confederacy.

General Halleck was not completely pleased with General Order 100. A month after the code was issued, Halleck gave the following guidance to General John Schofield, about to take command of U.S. forces in Missouri, a state plagued by endemic guerrilla warfare: "On this subject I commend to your careful attention the field instructions published in General Orders, No. 100, current series. These instructions have been most carefully considered before publication. Nevertheless, they are very imperfect, and as Missouri is peculiarly situated, many questions may arise which are not here alluded to."[54] Halleck was correct. The Lieber Code did not give clear guidance on some important problems (e.g., treatment of members of the enemy's regular army caught fighting in civilian clothing), and it contained a few grandiloquent statements that, taken out of context, could be construed as rejecting all limits on the conduct of war. The last sentence of article 5, for example—"To save the country is paramount to all other considerations"—in context refers to application of lawful security measures in occupied territory. Out of context, it can be taken as a sinister suggestion that law can be disregarded to save the country.[55] Despite its shortcomings, however, the Lieber Code remains the best summary of the laws and customs of war as they existed in the middle of the nineteenth century.

The influence of the Lieber Code survived, and even expanded, after the end of the Civil War. The code remained the official guidance on the law of war in the U.S. Army well into the twentieth century. It was influential in Europe, and in the 1870s it was adopted by the Prussian government for the guidance of its soldiers during the Franco-Prussian War, a particularly ironic development since Lieber had once fled Prussia as a political refugee. In 1899, the code was a major source for the drafters of the Hague Regulations on Land Warfare, the first multilateral treaty to attempt a comprehensive codification of the laws and customs of war. The 1899 Hague Regulations, in turn, formed the basis for the current four Geneva Conventions of 1949.

President Lincoln signed the Lieber Code as commander in chief of the army, but it appears he had no role in drafting it. Although he never cited the code in any of his speeches or writings, Lincoln almost certainly read it because, as he later noted in his public letter to James C. Conkling, the law of war provided the principal legal foundation for the Emancipation Proclamation and the president's other decisions on military treatment of enemy persons and property. Whether or not there was a direct influence, Lincoln's actions closely paralleled Lieber's words in two major respects.

The adoption of the principle of military necessity as a general standard for legitimate military action was one of the main reforms espoused by Francis Lieber in his code. As Chief Justice Marshall and

Justice Story had noted in *United States v. Brown*, under the laws of war as they were understood in 1812, governments were not required to respect any rights of the owner of private property belonging to an enemy national. By midcentury, there was a growing body of scholarly opinion that even in war property and other private rights should not be interfered with unless a valid military purpose—a military necessity—would be served. In his code for the U.S. Army, Lieber adopted this view:

> Military necessity, as understood by modern civilized nations, consists in the necessity of those measures which are indispensable for securing the ends of the war, and which are lawful according to the modern law and usages of war.
>
> Military necessity admits of all direct destruction of life or limb of armed enemies, and of other persons whose destruction is incidentally unavoidable in the armed contests of the war; it allows of the capturing of every armed enemy, and every enemy of importance to the hostile government, or of peculiar danger to the captor; it allows of all destruction of property, and . . . the appropriation of whatever an enemy's country affords necessary for the subsistence and safety of the army, and of such deception as does not involve the breaking of good faith.[56]

It should be noted that, both during the Civil War and in later nineteenth- and twentieth-century conflicts, the terms "necessity," "indispensable," and "unavoidable" were not taken literally by military commanders or their governments. In practice, so long as there was a rational connection, under circumstances as understood at the time, between an act of war and the defeat of the enemy's armed forces, the principle of military necessity was regarded as having been satisfied. President Lincoln expressed very similar ideas in his August 1863 letter to James C. Conkling when he wrote that "property, both of enemies and friends, may be taken when needed" and that it is needed "whenever taking it, helps us, or hurts the enemy."

A number of examples illustrate how loosely the concept of military necessity has been interpreted in practice. Shortly after the Civil War, the United States and Great Britain entered into negotiations to settle the claims of each nation against the other arising out of the war. During these negotiations, the British eventually conceded that Union destruction of cotton owned by British subjects was justified by military necessity, since the export of cotton was a primary economic support for the Confederate war effort.[57] Again, legal experts generally agree that it is permissible to destroy enemy lighthouses, despite their semi-humanitarian function, because they also contribute to maritime commerce with an enemy's ports.[58] More recently, Ethiopia and Eritrea established an international commission to adjudicate claims arising from a border war they waged between 1998 and 2000. One of Eritrea's claims was that the Ethiopian air force had illegally attacked a partially completed electric power plant that was not a legitimate military objective. The commission, however, agreed with Ethiopia "that electric power stations are generally recognized to be of sufficient importance to a State's capacity to meet its wartime needs of communication, transport and industry so as usually to qualify as military objectives during armed conflicts," and denied the Eritrean claim.[59] The destruction of cotton exports, lighthouses, and incomplete electric power plants are rarely "unavoidable" in a strict sense or "indispensable" to the victory of one side over the other. Nevertheless, each of these acts of war has been considered justified by military necessity.

Lieber was careful to explain that military necessity only authorized actions that were otherwise "lawful according to the modern law and usages of war," that is, that were not prohibited by some specific rule. Thus military necessity allowed the "direct destruction of life or limb of armed enemies" but only the capture of unarmed enemies. Lincoln expressed the same principle to Conkling when he wrote, "Civilized belligerents do all in their power to help themselves, or hurt the enemy, except a few things regarded as barbarous or cruel," such as "massacres of vanquished foes, and non-combatants, male and female." It should also be noted that in his final Emancipation Proclamation, Lincoln specifically mentioned "military necessity" as the primary justification for recognizing the freedom of slaves in Confederate territory.[60]

"Military necessity does not," the Lieber Code emphasized, "admit of cruelty—that is, the infliction of suffering for the sake of suffering or for revenge, nor of maiming or wounding except in fight, nor of torture to extort confessions."[61] As we will see in the following chapters, throughout the war, President Lincoln was continually concerned that military actions be undertaken only for valid military reasons, and never for motives of revenge or cruelty.

2

"Property, Both of Enemies and Friends, May Be Taken When Needed"

Seizure and Destruction of Civilian Property

One of Lincoln's earliest acts as commander in chief was to promise respect for the property of enemy civilians. In his proclamation of April 15, 1861, calling out 75,000 militia for federal service after the fall of Fort Sumter, the president deemed it proper to state that when these forces sought to repossess the forts, places, and property seized from the United States by the rebels, "the utmost care will be observed . . . to avoid any devastation; any destruction of, or interference with, property, or any disturbance of peaceful citizens, in any part of the country."[1] These assurances made a great deal of sense at that particular time.

In 1861, President Lincoln still believed that the majority of white Southerners were loyal to the Union, and that the seceding states had been led astray by a small cabal of secessionist fanatics. Also, before any major battle had even been fought, Confederate leaders were already claiming that Union soldiers would engage in widespread atrocities, so the president was prudent to reassure the (presumably loyal) majority of civilians in the Confederate States that their lands and other property would not be at risk from the federal militia.[2] In particular, the reference to "interference" with property would be understood as a commitment not to meddle with the institution of slavery. The rebellious people of the South were still U.S. citizens, and their property was protected by the Fifth Amendment, which forbade government taking of private property without "just compensation."

This promise of extreme restraint remained the official position of the Lincoln administration for more than a year, until the summer of 1862. However, as the scale of the war widened and intensified it became clear that peacetime protections for private property could not be strictly applied in the midst of operations over hundreds of square miles involving tens of thousands of soldiers on each side. As noted in the introduction, Civil War armies were inherently destructive of nearby civilian property.

Beyond this, legitimate operations necessarily impinged on civilian property. President Lincoln recognized this reality in a letter to Senator Orville Browning in September 1861: "If a commanding General finds a necessity to seize the farm of a private owner, for a pasture, an encampment, or a fortification, he has the right to do so, and to so hold it, as long as the necessity lasts; . . . this is within military law, because within military necessity."[3]

Between July 1861 and July 1862, the president witnessed a frustrating mixture of victories and defeats. In 1861, Union arms had been humiliated at the battles of Bull Run and Ball's Bluff. General George McClellan had successfully driven the Confederates out of the western, pro-Union counties of Virginia, but had been reluctant to take the offensive when placed in command of the Army of the Potomac.

Lincoln had long believed that slavery was contrary to divine and natural law, and that it was on the road to inevitable extinction so long as it was confined to its existing geographical limits. During this time of frustration, however, Lincoln began to doubt these long-held beliefs. If Providence was against the expansion of slavery, why were the Confederate armies so uniformly triumphant? Senator Orville Browning later recalled telling the president at about this time that the United States could not "hope for the blessing of God on the efforts of our armies, until we strike a decisive blow at the institution of slavery." "Browning," Lincoln replied, "suppose God is against us in our view on the subject of slavery in this country, and our method of dealing with it?" The senator was "much impressed by his reply, because it caused me to reflect that perhaps he had thought more deeply on this subject than I had."[4]

Things appeared brighter in early 1862. The fall of Forts Henry and Donelson in February led to Union occupation of most of Kentucky and Tennessee. In March, General McClellan finally began to move against Richmond in the Peninsular Campaign. Frustration and defeat returned in late spring. At the end of June, Robert E. Lee's Army of Northern Virginia threw McClellan back from the outskirts of Richmond to Harrison's Landing on the James River. In the West, the Union army became bogged down in the seemingly endless siege of Corinth, Mississippi.

This time, however, Lincoln did not react with despair. General McClellan had been a strong advocate of a "soft war" policy that protected civilian property and preserved the social system of the slave states. Perhaps Orville Browning had been right—God would not bless the Union cause with victory as long as McClellan's policies remained in place. Public opinion in the North was also becoming increasingly frustrated with policies that protected the inhabitants of the slave states against any interference with their "peculiar institution."[5]

Other influences were at work as well. On June 23, 1862, the president traveled to New York City to consult with Winfield Scott, who had retired as commanding general of the army the previous fall. From late June through mid-July, Major General John Pope, called East from Missouri to command the newly formed Army of Virginia, also acted as an informal military adviser to Lincoln. One of the president-elect's escorts on the journey from Springfield to Washington, Pope had gained Lincoln's confidence as one of the few strongly antislavery officers of the regular army. In 1861–1862, faced with endemic guerrilla warfare in Missouri, he had adopted "hard war" measures to discourage civilian support for Confederate irregulars, and advocated similar measures for the war in the East.[6]

On June 28, General John Pope took command of the Army of Virginia, formed from Union forces in Northern Virginia and elements of the Army of the Potomac evacuated from the Virginia Peninsula. After McClellan's debacle in front of the Confederate capital, Pope's task was to advance on Richmond by marching directly south from Washington, an approach the president had always preferred to McClellan's amphibious campaign. This route would take the Army of Virginia through almost 100 miles of hostile territory, and on July 18 General Pope issued a series of general orders on the treatment of civilians in his area of operations.[7] Some of these measures, especially those aimed at preventing espionage and sabotage, later became quite controversial. One order specifically dealt with treatment of private property:

Hereafter, as far as practicable, the troops of this command will subsist upon the country in which their operations are carried on. In all cases supplies for this purpose will be taken by the officers to whose department they properly belong under the orders of the commanding officer of the troops for whose use they are intended. Vouchers will be given to the owners, stating on their face that they will be payable at the conclusion of the war, upon sufficient testimony being furnished that such owners have been loyal citizens of the United States since the date of the vouchers. Whenever it is known that supplies can be furnished in any district of the country where the troops are to operate the use of trains for carrying subsistence will be dispensed with as far as possible.[8]

General Pope appears to have consulted with Lincoln before issuing general orders for his campaign.[9] Four days after Pope issued an order to live off the land in Virginia, the president adopted a similar policy for all his armies.

On July 21, 1862, the president called a surprise cabinet meeting in which he announced that he had become "profoundly concerned at the present aspect of affairs, and had determined to take some definitive steps in respect to military action and slavery."[10] Slavery would be taken up the next day, when he read the cabinet his first draft of the Emancipation Proclamation. On July 21, however, Lincoln proposed to deal with the broader issue of enemy civilian property. The president had drafted three military orders for the cabinet to consider:

1.

Ordered, that Military commanders within the States of Virginia, South Carolina, Georgia, Florida, Alabama, Mississippi, Louisiana, Texas, and Arkansas, in an orderly manner, seize and use any property, real or personal, which may be necessary or convenient for their several commands as supplies, or for other military purposes; and that while property may be destroyed for proper military objects, none shall be destroyed in wantonness or malice.

2.

That, military and Naval commanders shall employ as laborers, within and from said States, so many persons of African descent as can be advantageously used for military and naval purposes, giving them reasonable wages for their labor.

3.

That, as to both property and persons of African descent, accounts shall be kept sufficiently accurate and in detail to show quantities and amounts, and from whom both property and such persons shall have come, as a basis upon which compensation can be made in proper cases; and the several Departments of this Government shall attend to and perform their appropriate parts toward the execution of these orders.[11]

Treasury Secretary Salmon P. Chase recorded that, after a "good deal of discussion" in the cabinet, the first order was "universally approved," the second "approved entirely," and the third approved by all except himself. He correctly "doubted the expediency of attempting to keep accounts" for the benefit of inhabitants of hostile areas.[12] The presidential order was formally sent to the secretary of war on July 22.

Confederate private property would now be treated in accordance with the international laws of war, not the Fifth Amendment to the Constitution.[13] The third order held out the possibility of compensation for property seized or destroyed by the military, but made no promise in that regard. Congress might grant compensation to loyal owners, or even to some of those who supported the rebellion, but that was a matter of legislative grace to be decided in the future. To put this decision into proper context, it should be noted that a policy of making compensation conditional on the loyalty of property owners did not originate with President Lincoln or General Pope. In August 1861, the Confederate cavalry leader Turner Ashby had seized the stores of A. R. McQuilken, a pro-Union shopkeeper in Berkeley County, Virginia. The Confederate military authorities in Richmond ruled that his action should be "regarded as a seizure from the enemy," and that the property "may be turned over to the quartermaster and hospital departments for use."[14] In December, Confederate secretary of war Judah Benjamin, in response to reports that some Virginians were exacting "exorbitant prices" for supplies sold to the army, directed General Joseph Johnston to regard such persons as disloyal and to seize the goods without compensation:

This state of things should not be tolerated. Our Army must be fed. The supplies necessary for this purpose must be had, and those who refuse to sell them to the Government at fair and reasonable rates cannot be regarded as true friends of our cause. You are, therefore, requested to issue orders requiring the impressment of such supplies, wherever the owners refuse to dispose of them at fair market value in Confederate money. It is hoped, however, that the knowledge that such orders have been issued will prevent the necessity of executing them, otherwise the exigencies of our Army demand that they be promptly enforced.[15]

Although General Pope had anticipated the July 22 order in the eastern theater of war, it was not rigorously applied in the West until the end of the year. There it would lead to major changes in the way the war was waged. As part of General Grant's campaign to capture Vicksburg, Mississippi, his army was operating in the central part of that state, with his headquarters at Oxford, in December 1862. He recalled in his memoirs:

Up to this time it had been regarded as an axiom in war that large bodies of troops must operate from a base of supplies which they always covered and guarded in all forward movements. . . . By my orders, and in accordance with previous instructions from Washington, all the forage within reach was collected under the supervision of the chief quartermaster and the provisions under the chief commissary, receipts being given when there was any one to take them; the supplies in any event to be accounted for as government stores. The stock was bountiful, but still it gave me no idea of the possibility of supplying a moving column in an enemy's country from the country itself.[16]

Then, on December 20, Confederate raiders under General Earl Van Dorn destroyed Grant's main supply base at Holly Springs and tore up the railroad that would have been used for new supplies. After the raid, some citizens of Oxford came to Grant "with broad smiles on their faces indicating intense joy, to ask what I was going to do now without anything for my soldiers to eat." In fact, Grant had already taken measures to redress the situation:

After sending cavalry to drive Van Dorn away, my next order was to dispatch all the wagons we had, under proper escort, to collect and bring in all supplies of forage and food from a region of fifteen miles east and west of the road from our front back to Grand Junction, leaving two months' supplies for the families of those whose stores were taken. I was amazed at the quantity of supplies the country afforded. It showed that we could have subsisted off the country for two months instead of two weeks without going beyond the limits designated. This taught me a lesson which was taken advantage of later in the campaign, when our army lived twenty days with the issue of only five days' rations by the commissary.[17]

In 1864, General William Sherman would apply this lesson in the Meridian campaign and, more famously, in his march from Atlanta to the sea and through the Carolinas.

In the mid-nineteenth century, international law on the protection of private property in war was in a state of flux. The older view was that in warfare on land, all private property of enemy civilians could be seized or destroyed by enemy armed forces without compensation.[18] More modern legal authorities argued that private property should in general be respected and protected by warring armies, subject to certain exceptions.

The recognized exceptions, however, could be so broad that they left little protection in practice. In 1836, Henry Wheaton, the first American to write a book on international law, stated: "Private property on land is . . . exempt from confiscation, with the exception of such as may become booty in special cases, when taken from enemies in the field or in besieged towns, and of military contributions levied upon the inhabitants of hostile territory."[19] Wheaton's statement that private property could become lawful booty "in besieged towns" was a delicately worded reference to the ancient custom of allowing soldiers to pillage fortified towns taken by assault.[20] During the siege of Vera Cruz, Winfield Scott argued that bombardment of the town would be more humane than taking it by assault because of the danger to civilians posed by pillaging soldiers. Pillage was banned in the U.S. Army by the Lieber Code, although enforcement of the ban was often lax or nonexistent.[21] Pillage was not formally prohibited by treaty until 1899.[22]

In practice, authorized foraging activities often became pillaging expeditions, particularly when soldiers, whether Union or Confederate, operated out of sight of their officers in the midst of a hostile population. The looting conducted by General Sherman's "bummers" in Georgia and the Carolinas is legendary, but it was not unique. In a letter to her parents, Elizabeth Beach of Mississippi described how General Benjamin Grierson's foragers had looted the property belonging to her and her husband, Asa:

> All day working like ants, all over the house up stairs and down, in every hole and corner, searching and peeping every where, [the soldiers] carried off every [Irish potato,] beet[,] onion[,] beans [and] even took time to pick pans of beans[.] [They] took my pillow cases to put them in[,] took towels[,] one new table cloth[,] all my knives but 3[,] some of my dishes and every pan they could find. Took my shears and Asa[']s hatchet. Tore my house all to pieces it would take me a week to mess it up like they did, pulled all our dirty clothes out of the closets, and examined them. Took all of Asa's clothes they could find. . . .
>
> They did not take any of my clothes, except pocket hand-kerchiefs. Sarah & me both had some new handkerchiefs, they got them all, and would have taken our dresses, if we had not fought over them so[.] [A]s they pulled them out, I would take them from them and throw them to Sarah, [and] she would sit on them [until] she had a large pile under her[.] [S]he said she would fight over them a long time before they got them.[23]

As an alternative to authorized pillage, the practice of levying of "military contributions" was developed in the seventeenth century. One historian defined contributions as "war taxes imposed on an area, city, town, village or even an estate by an occupying, passing or threatening army," and noted that customarily "the sanction imposed against those who refused to pay was fire."[24] During the United States war with Mexico, for example, General Winfield Scott imposed a contribution of $150,000 on Mexico City.[25] Part of this money was used to establish the Soldiers' Home in Washington, D.C., later a favorite summer retreat for President Lincoln and his family.[26]

By authorizing "commanders within the States of Virginia, South Carolina, Georgia, Florida, Alabama, Mississippi, Louisiana, Texas, and Arkansas" to "seize and use any property . . . which may be necessary or convenient for their several commands as supplies," President Lincoln authorized the army to levy contributions in kind—food, forage, and other military supplies—on civilians in those states. During the Civil

War the Union did not levy monetary contributions in hostile areas. (Any substantial contribution would probably have been paid in Confederate money, and under no circumstances would the Lincoln administration recognize the legitimacy of currency issued by that source.)

On occasion, Confederate commanders demanded monetary contributions from pro-Union towns. General Jubal Early is a notable example. Before his 1864 attack on Washington, Early collected $200,000 from Frederick, Maryland, and his subordinate, General John McCausland, raised a $20,000 contribution from Hagerstown, Maryland. McCausland also demanded $5,000 from the Maryland hamlet of Middletown, but settled for $1,500. On a raid into the North later in 1864, McCausland, acting under Early's orders, demanded $100,000 in gold or $500,000 in greenbacks from Chambersburg, Pennsylvania. On July 30, 1864, in accordance with military custom, Chambersburg was put to the torch when its citizens could not comply with the levy.[27]

Aside from imposing contributions in kind on a hostile civilian population, for what "other military purposes" could private property be legitimately seized or destroyed under the president's order of July 22, 1862? The 1863 Lieber Code restated the 1862 order in terms of "military necessity," but it did little to clarify exactly what was permitted or prohibited by that standard:

> Military necessity . . . allows of all destruction of property, and obstruction of the ways and channels of traffic, travel, or communication, and of all withholding of sustenance or means of life from the enemy; [and] of the appropriation of whatever an enemy's country affords necessary for the subsistence and safety of the army. . . .
>
> Private property, unless forfeited by crimes or by offenses of the owner, can be seized only by way of military necessity, for the support or other benefit of the army or of the United States.[28]

After approving the Lieber Code, President Lincoln issued no further general guidance on the treatment of enemy property during the last two years of the war. He did, however, intervene when specific instances of abuse or injustice were brought to his attention. One such case produced Lincoln's most extended and mature reflections on private property and the limits of military necessity. Mrs. Mary Morton's home had been seized by an army provost marshal in Arkansas, and somehow she appealed directly to President Lincoln in early 1865. Bypassing the military chain of command, the president wrote directly to Major General Joseph Reynolds, in command of the Department of Arkansas, to give him a short course on the law of war and private property:

> It would appear . . . that Mrs. Mary E. Morton is the owner, independently of her husband, of a certain building, premises and furniture, which she, with her children, has been occupying and using peaceably during the war, until recently, when the Provost-Marshal has, in the name of the U.S. Government, seized the whole of said property, and ejected her from it. It also appears by her statement to me, that her husband went off in the rebellion at the beginning, wherein he still remains.
>
> It would seem that this seizure has not been made for any military object, as for a place of storage, a hospital, or the like, because this would not have required the seizure of the furniture, and especially not the return of furniture previously taken away.
>
> The seizure must have been on some claim of confiscation, a matter of which the courts, and not the Provost-Marshals, or other military officers, are to judge. In this very case, would probably be the questions: "Is either the husband or wife a traitor?" "Does the property belong to the husband or to the wife?" "Is the property of the wife confiscable for the treason of the husband?" and other similar questions, all which it is ridiculous for a Provost-Marshal to assume to decide.
>
> The true rule for the military, is to seize such property as is needed for Military uses and reasons, and let the rest alone. Cotton and other staple articles of commerce are seizable for Military reasons; Dwelling-houses and furniture are seldom so. If Mrs. Morton is playing traitor, to the extent of practical injury, seize her, but leave her house to the courts.—Please revise and adjust this case upon these principles.[29]

After the war, Lincoln's statement that cotton was a legitimate object of seizure for military reasons received support from an unexpected quarter. Some of the cotton burned by Federal troops during the Civil War belonged to British subjects, and in the 1870s the government of the United Kingdom claimed compensation from the United States for the destruction of neutral private property. Eventually, however, rather than go to neutral arbitration on the issue, the British government accepted the American argument that the destruction was justified by military necessity because cotton was the South's principal export and the source of most of the Confederacy's foreign arms and military supplies, and all but one of the claims were dropped. The exception involved an incident in an area under the firm control of the Union army at the time of the destruction.[30] Lincoln, a strong believer in peaceful resolution of international disputes, would have been doubly pleased.

Though not openly stated in the president's letter to General Reynolds, it seems clear that Lincoln suspected that Mary Morton's house and furniture had been confiscated to punish her husband for his Confederate service, and not for any valid military reason. This would be a continuing concern of his throughout the war. He had concluded his order of July 22, 1862, allowing Federal armies to live off the land, by stating that "property may be destroyed for proper military objects, none shall be destroyed in wantonness or malice." This was typical Lincoln. All his life he had worried that violent emotions—"malice"—would overcome the forces of reason, whether in the form of lynch mobs in St. Louis, Missouri, and Alton, Illinois, or of angry soldiers burning the home of a notorious secessionist. Early in his public life he proposed "cold, calculating unimpassioned reason" as the best defense for America's free institutions, and as president he continued to base his personal and political philosophy on reason.[31] Throughout the Civil War, forestalling or reversing military actions motivated by revenge or other malice would be a priority for the president. Military actions must be based on rational military judgment, not emotion. As he noted to General Reynolds, confiscation of "Dwelling-houses and furniture" could seldom be justified as a legitimate military act. The same was true of military attempts to manage religious property.

When Lincoln learned, in December 1862, that military authorities in Missouri had ordered Samuel McPheeters, minister at the Vine Street Presbyterian Church in St. Louis, to leave the state because of his disloyal sentiments, he suspended the order. Major General Samuel R. Curtis, the Union commander in Missouri, protested that McPheeters was "evidently a bad rebel doing injury here," and that "rebel priests are dangerous and diabolical." As to McPheeters's church, Curtis explained: "There is a union and secession party in his congregation, and union men side with the union side, and the peace of society seems to require a conclusion of such strife in favor of the loyal side of the question."[32] This statement implied that the military authorities had intervened in a dispute within the church congregation, placing the "loyal" faction in control of the church in addition to exiling the disloyal clergyman. Lincoln replied that since General Curtis was the man on the scene, he would defer to his judgment on the need to exile McPheeters, but strongly cautioned him against intervening in internal disputes over control of a church: "I must add that the U.S. government must not, as by this order, undertake to run the churches. When an individual, in a church or out of it, becomes dangerous to the public interest, he must be checked; but let the churches, as such take care of themselves. It will not do for the U.S. to appoint Trustees, Supervisors, or other agents for the churches."[33]

The president quickly discovered that once the military had intervened in the church dispute, it was not an easy matter to extract the government from it. General Curtis informed President Lincoln that he had allowed Reverend McPheeters to remain in St. Louis and that his orders had been modified to avoid any inference that the government was intervening in internal church disputes: "The Reverend Gentleman has been allowed to remain in the city, suspended from the exercise of any public functions on the ground of his disloyalty."[34] However, suspension from the exercise of public functions meant that Reverend McPheeters could not preach in his own church.

Over the next year, Lincoln received numerous petitions and communications on the status and treatment of the Reverend Dr. McPheeters from General Curtis and both the pro- and anti-McPheeters factions of the congregation. In December 1863, he replied to one such petition with evident frustration and disgust:

> I have just looked over a petition signed by some three dozen citizens of St-Louis, and three accompanying letters, one by yourself, one by a Mr. Nathan Ranney, and one by a Mr. John D. Coalter, the whole relating to the Rev. Dr. McPheeters. The petition prays, in the name of justice and mercy, that I will restore Dr. McPheeters to all his Ecclesiastical rights. This gives no intimation as to what Ecclesiastical rights are withheld. . . .
>
> Now, all this sounds very strangely, and withal, a little as if you gentlemen making the application do not understand the

case alike; one affirming that the Dr. is enjoying all the rights of a civilian, and another pointing out to me what will secure his *release!* . . .

I have never interfered, nor thought of interfering as to who shall or shall not preach in any Church; nor have I knowingly or believingly, tolerated any one else to so interfere by my authority. If any one is so interfering, by color of my authority, I would like to have it specifically made known to me.

If, after all, what is now sought, is to have me put Dr. Mc[Pheeters] back, over the heads of a majority of his own Congregation, that too, will be declined. I will not have control of any church, on any side.[35]

In 1864, the president was dragged into another ecclesiastical morass, this time involving a church in Memphis, Tennessee. When that state was under Confederate control, the congregation of the Second Presbyterian Church fired their minister for his loyalty to the Union and voted to dedicate the church bell to Confederate general P. G. T. Beauregard. After Memphis was occupied by Union forces, General Sherman restored the minister to his pulpit and placed the church under control of pro-Union trustees. The ousted trustees then petitioned President Lincoln, and he responded much as he had in the St. Louis case:

I have written before and now repeat the U S Government must not undertake to run the Churches. When an individual in a church or out of it becomes dangerous to the public interest he must be checked, but the churches as such must take care of themselves. It will not do for the U.S. to appoint trustees supervisors or other agents for the churches. I add if the military have military need of the church building let them keep it; otherwise let them get out of it, and leave it and its owners alone except for causes that justify the arrest of anyone.[36]

In response to this communication from the president, the military authorities in Memphis returned the Second Presbyterian Church to control of the old trustees.

Naturally enough, the pro-Union trustees installed by General Sherman then approached the president themselves. He forwarded their petition back to the U.S. commander on the scene, General Cadwallader Washburn, with this endorsement:

> I am now told that the military were not in possession of the building, and yet that in pretended obedience to the [March 4, 1864, instructions] they, the military put one set of men out of, and another set into the building. This, if true, is more extraordinary. I say again, if there be no military need for the building leave it alone, neither putting any one in, or out of it except on finding some one preaching or practicing treason, in which case lay hands upon him, just as if he was doing the same thing in any other building, or in the streets or highways.[37]

On June 22, General Washburn, understandably perplexed, requested additional guidance from the president. Did President Lincoln's endorsement mean that he should oust the current trustees of the church and restore the pro-Union group, or should he do nothing? At this point President Lincoln washed his hands of the whole thing. John Hay, the president's secretary, notated on General Washburn's letter the statement, "President declines making any further order in case of Presbyt[eria]n Church in Memphis."[38]

Meanwhile, unbeknown to the president, in November 1863 Secretary of War Edwin Stanton issued a circular letter authorizing Edward R. Ames, a pro-Union Methodist bishop, to take control of Methodist churches in the South that did not have clergy loyal to the Union.[39] John Hogan, a Methodist minister in St. Louis who knew Abraham Lincoln from the time they had both served in the Illinois legislature, brought this circular letter to the president's attention in February 1864. As a denomination, the Methodists had been among the administration's staunchest supporters in the North.[40] Stanton therefore probably thought the Ames circular was a noncontroversial reward for a group of Union loyalists, and that there was no need to bother the president about the issue.

President Lincoln, however, immediately wrote to Secretary Stanton explaining the position he had taken in the McPheeters case. The concluding paragraph is a rare written expression of presidential irritation with his secretary of war: "After having made these declarations in good faith, and in writing, you can conceive of my embarrassment at now having brought to me what purports to be a formal order of the

War Department, bearing date Nov. 30th 1863, giving Bishop Ames control and possession of all the Methodist churches in certain Southern Military Departments, whose pastors have not been appointed by a loyal Bishop or Bishops, and ordering the military to aid him against any resistance which may be made to his taking such possession and control—What is to be done about it?"[41] Two days later Lincoln informed John Hogan that the order had been modified to exclude Missouri from its application. The president explained that it never applied to Kentucky, "nor, as I learn from the Secretary, was it ever intended for any more than a means of rallying the Methodist people in favor of the Union, in localities where the rebellion had disorganized and scattered them." The president was still unhappy with the order, fearing it was subject to abuse, but, perhaps to avoid embarrassment to Secretary Stanton and Bishop Ames, "it is not quite easy to withdraw it entirely, and at once."[42]

In retrospect it seems strange that after signing the Lieber Code in April 1863, Abraham Lincoln never again gave general guidance to his officers on the treatment of civilian property. He was willing to intervene when specific wrongs were brought to his attention, but no new presidential orders were issued setting out when dwelling houses could and could not legitimately be seized. He would act to stop military interference with specific churches in St. Louis and Memphis, but never sent a presidential order to all his commanders, or even to his secretary of war, stating flatly that the military must not undertake to run churches. Two months after confronting Stanton on the issue in February 1864, the president still found it necessary to issue a "suggestion" to the commanding general of the Department of the Missouri that he should not require church members to take a loyalty oath as a condition for attending services: "I have found that men who have not even been suspected of disloyalty, are very averse to taking an oath of any sort as a condition, to exercising an ordinary right of citizenship." The president also noted the anomaly that "while men may without an oath, assemble in a noisy political meeting, they must take the oath, to assemble in a religious meeting."[43]

Lincoln did propose a broad protection for dwelling houses on one occasion. During his 1864 campaign in the Shenandoah Valley of Virginia, Union general David Hunter ordered the burning of several private residences in retaliation for Confederate guerrilla activity, including the Lexington home of John Letcher, a former governor of Virginia.

In the course of Jubal Early's campaign against Washington in July of that year, the residence of the Maryland's governor, Augustus Bradford, was burned by Confederate cavalry in retaliation for the destruction of Letcher's house. Hunter thereafter ordered more house burnings in retaliation for the destruction of Bradford's home. In retaliation for these acts, General Early ordered General McCausland to raid into southern Pennsylvania and demand a monetary contribution from the town of Chambersburg. If the town was unable to pay, he was to burn it. In compliance with these orders, McCausland set fire to Chambersburg on July 30, 1864, destroying about half the town.

Clearly things had gotten out of hand. On August 14, 1864, President Lincoln sent a telegram to General Grant proposing an end to the burning of houses by both sides: "The Secretary of War and I concur that you had better confer with Gen. Lee and stipulate for a mutual discontinuance of house-burning and other destruction of private property. The time and manner of conference, and particulars of stipulation we leave, on our part, to your convenience and judgment."[44] The negotiations had to be conducted through Grant and Lee because, according to custom, military-to-military agreements between opposing commanders had no political implications. An agreement concluded directly between the governments in Washington and Richmond, however, could be considered a form of official recognition of the Confederate States of America as a legitimate political entity.

Grant had reason to feel uneasy about this telegram. What was it—an order or advice? What "other destruction of private property" should or could be covered? In addition, based on personal experience, Grant was skeptical of the value of military-to-military agreements with the Confederate military.

A year earlier, Grant had captured about 29,000 Confederate officers and men when Vicksburg, Mississippi, surrendered. Of these prisoners, 23,000 were "paroled" and released.[45] Parole was an agreement between a prisoner of war and his captor. The prisoner, in exchange for freedom or less restrictive conditions of captivity, promised not to engage in specified activity, such as renewed military service in the war or attempting to escape. This promise was often put in writing and signed by the prisoner or, if an entire unit was being paroled, by the commanding officer.[46] Under a military-to-military agreement concluded in 1862, Federal and Confederate officials known as Agents of Exchange were to trade lists of prisoners each side had paroled and were then to exchange discharges from paroles allowing an equivalent number of men on each side to return to military duty.[47]

When Confederate general Joseph E. Johnston informed President Jefferson Davis of the fall of Vicksburg, he noted that the paroled Confederate soldiers were demoralized after their defeat and did not want to be sent to a special camp for parolees. Davis replied that "there will be no need to detain the men in a paroled camp, as we shall insist on immediate discharge [from their paroles], and give to them an opportunity again to serve their country" without waiting for an official exchange of lists through the Agents of Exchange.[48] General Grant and other U.S. officials regarded this unilateral discharge from parole of the Vicksburg prisoners as an act of bad faith by the Confederates.[49]

Rather than start negotiations with Lee over house burning, Grant therefore made a counterproposal. On August 17, he telegraphed the president that he had "thought over your dispatch relative to an arrangement between Gen. Lee and myself for the suppression of insindiaryism" by both armies. "Experience has taught us," he went on, "that agreements made with rebels are binding upon us but are not observed by them longer than suits their convenience." As an alternative he proposed that the U.S. Army issue an order prohibiting the burning of private property except out of military necessity or as an act of retaliation for similar action by the Confederates. The order could limit retaliatory burning to cases approved by the commanding general of an army or a military district. "I could publish the order or it could be published by you. This is respectfully submitted for your consideration and I will then act as you deem best."[50]

No order such as Grant suggested was ever issued by the president, the War Department, or General Grant. After April 1863, President Lincoln remained reluctant to issue general instructions on the treatment of enemy private property, even when suggested by the commanding general he had personally selected. After Chambersburg, however, enthusiasm for burning the homes of their enemies declined on both sides. Perhaps the president thought that further action to curtail it was no longer required.

3

"Strong Measures, Deemed Indispensable but Harsh at Best"

Retaliation and Guerrilla Warfare

Most of the house burning that bothered the president had been carried out, by both sides, as acts of "retaliation." In theory, each was a response to a violation of the laws and customs of war by the other side, intended to deter future violations. Article 27 of the Lieber Code expressed the prevailing view: "The law of war can no more wholly dispense with retaliation than can the law of nations, of which it is a branch. Yet civilized nations acknowledge retaliation as the sternest feature of war. A reckless enemy often leaves to his opponent no other means of securing himself against the repetition of barbarous outrage." Retaliation is the "sternest feature of war" because it necessarily inflicts punishment on the innocent rather than the guilty. Acts of retaliation cause innocent civilians or prisoners of war to lose their property, their freedom, and perhaps their lives as a means of persuading a guilty enemy to cease acts that the retaliating party regards as violations of the laws and customs of war. Perhaps out of Victorian delicacy, Francis Lieber did not make this explicit. The U.S. Army's official guidance on the law of war in 1914 was more blunt: "Persons guilty of no offense whatever may be punished as retaliation for the guilty acts of others."[1]

Two highly effective acts of retaliation by the Confederacy—one threatened, the other executed—illustrate how the practice was supposed to work. The issue in both cases was whether certain Confederate combatants were entitled to be treated as prisoners of war.

Prisoner of war status was important because only uniformed soldiers and other legitimate belligerents were entitled to it. Legitimate belligerents cannot, under the laws and customs of war, be punished for military actions against the enemy that under peacetime criminal law would be murder and mayhem, such as killing enemy soldiers or sailors in combat. As one Civil War general explained to his officers in early 1862, "a soldier duly enrolled and authorized to act in a military capacity in the enemy's service is not . . . individually responsible for the taking of human life in battle, siege, etc."[2] The Lieber Code stressed the importance for individual soldiers of being accorded prisoner of war status:

> A prisoner of war is subject to no punishment for being a public enemy, nor is any revenge wreaked upon him by the intentional infliction of any suffering, or disgrace, by cruel imprisonment, want of food, by mutilation, death, or any other barbarity.
> So soon as a man is armed by a sovereign government and takes the soldier's oath of fidelity, he is a belligerent; his killing, wounding, or other warlike acts are not individual crimes or offenses.[3]

Early in the Civil War, the Lincoln administration decided that captured members of the regular Confederate army would be treated as prisoners of war. War at sea was a different matter, however. On April 19, 1861, President Lincoln signed a proclamation declaring a blockade of seaports in the rebel states.[4] As discussed in chapter 1, the proclamation also declared that anyone acting "under the pretended authority" of the Confederate government to capture or molest merchant ships flying the U.S. flag would "be held amenable to the laws of the United States for the prevention and punishment of piracy." The stage was set for a confrontation over U.S. treatment of captured crewmen from Confederate privateers.

On July 6, 1861, the schooner *Enchantress* from Boston was captured by the Confederate privateer *Jeff Davis*, sailing out of Charleston, South Carolina. In accordance with custom, the crew of the *Enchantress* was transferred to the *Jeff Davis* to be held prisoner until they could be safely released on neutral territory or to a neutral ship. There was one exception—James Garrick, the ship's cook, a free African American. Confederate lieutenant William Smith, commander of the prize crew that took possession of *Enchantress*, was overheard to remark that Garrick would "fetch $1,500 when we get him into Charleston." Garrick would be sold as a slave in Charleston, presumably without even the questionable benefit of a prize court hearing.

On July 22, however, the *Enchantress* was stopped on its voyage back to Charleston by the U.S. warship *Albatross*. Lieutenant Smith and his crew tried to bluff their way out of the situation by pretending to be the original Boston crew of the *Enchantress*, but Garrick, risking his life to retain his freedom, jumped into the North Atlantic and swam toward the federal warship yelling that the schooner was in the hands of the Confederates. Smith, his crew, and the *Enchantress* were soon in the custody of the U.S. Navy and were sent to Philadelphia. In accordance with presidential policy, on October 22, 1861, Lieutenant Smith was tried and convicted of piracy by the U.S. District Court in Philadelphia and sentenced to hang.[5]

The United States now found itself in the strange position of treating Confederates captured on land as prisoners of war while punishing many of those captured at sea as pirates. The Lincoln administration nevertheless intended to carry out its policy on privateers. However, the Confederate government had issued a warning that if any of its officers or sailors were executed as pirates, it would hang a Union prisoner of similar rank.[6] After Lieutenant Smith was sentenced, Colonel Michael Corcoran of the Sixty-ninth New York State Militia, who was captured at the First Battle of Bull Run, was selected by lot and moved to a death cell pending the outcome of the controversy. The Sixty-ninth was an Irish American unit, and Corcoran was a power in the New York Democratic Party. The last thing President Lincoln needed was to give the New York Democrats a new reason to oppose the administration's war policies.

In an effort to settle the crisis, the U.S. government made a number of compromise proposals, such as directly exchanging Lieutenant Smith for Colonel Corcoran, but the Confederates were adamant—their privateers must be treated as prisoners of war, now and in the future. By January 1862, the Lincoln administration had capitulated completely to Confederate demands. It officially recognized Lieutenant Smith as a prisoner of war and dropped the policy of treating as pirates Confederate officers involved in raiding Union commerce. Colonel Corcoran survived, but the threat of retaliation against him had worked.

Three years later, Confederate lieutenant colonel John Singleton Mosby carried out a grim but effective act of retaliation in Virginia. The issue was whether the men of his command, the Forty-third Virginia Cavalry Battalion, popularly known as "Mosby's Rangers," were to be treated as prisoners of war or punished as unlawful belligerents.

Under the laws and customs of war, not every fighter is entitled to be treated as a prisoner of war on capture. At the time of the Civil War, members of armed groups who were not authorized by the United States, the Confederate States, or the government of an individual state, and who posed as civilians when not fighting, were not lawful belligerents and could be punished if captured: "Men, or squads of men, who commit hostilities, whether by fighting, or inroads for destruction or plunder, or by raids of any kind, without commission, without being part and portion of the organized hostile army, and without sharing continuously in the war, but who do so with intermitting returns to their homes and avocations, or with the occasional assumption of the semblance of peaceful pursuits, divesting themselves of the character or appearance of soldiers . . . , are not entitled to the privileges of prisoners of war, but shall be treated summarily as highway robbers or pirates."[7] In the fall of 1861, for example, the Confederate War Department ordered that East Tennessee civilians loyal to the Union who had burned railroad bridges used by the Confederate army were "to be tried summarily by drum-head court-martial, and, if found guilty, executed on the spot by hanging," adding that "it would be well to leave their bodies hanging in the vicinity of the burned bridges."[8]

In addition, even members of the regular armed forces could be treated as unlawful belligerents if they were caught engaging hostilities or spying while in civilian clothing or in the enemy's uniform. On this basis, pro-Confederate bridge burners in Missouri faced the same fate as the Unionist bridge burners in Tennessee. Confederate general Sterling Price protested to Union general Henry Halleck that "individuals and parties of men specially appointed and instructed by me to destroy railroads, culverts and bridges by tearing them up, burning, &c., have been arrested and subjected to a general court-martial for alleged crimes which all the laws of warfare heretofore recognized by the civilized world have regarded as distinctly lawful and proper." Halleck shot back that anyone destroying property while posing as a civilian was not a lawful combatant, even if the acts were authorized by his government:

If you send armed forces wearing the garb of soldiers and duly organized and enrolled as legitimate belligerents to destroy railroads, bridges, &c., as a military act we shall kill them if possible in open warfare, or if we capture them we shall treat them as prisoners of war. But it is well understood that you have sent numbers of your adherents in the garb of peaceful citizens and under false pretenses through our lines into Northern Missouri to . . . burn and destroy railroad bridges thus endangering the lives of thousands. . . . You certainly will not pretend that men guilty of such crimes although "specially appointed and instructed" by you are entitled to the rights and immunities of ordinary prisoners of war. If you do will you refer me to a single authority on the laws of war which recognizes such a claim?[9]

According to the Lieber Code, the law of war regarded "partisans" as lawful belligerents, "entitled to all the privileges of the prisoner of war." "Partisans" were defined as "soldiers armed and wearing the uniform of their army, but belonging to a corps which acts detached from the main body for the purpose of making inroads into the territory occupied by the enemy."[10] Mosby's Rangers were organized under the Confederate States Partisan Ranger Act, generally wore uniform in action, and were subject to the jurisdiction of Confederate courts-martial. Organizationally, the Forty-third Battalion was part of Lee's Army of Northern Virginia. The soldiers did not receive regular pay, but, like privateers in sea warfare, were to be compensated for property captured from the U.S. government.[11] They were clearly partisans under the Lieber Code and entitled to prisoner of war treatment on capture.

Mosby's men operated in Virginia. In the western theater of war, however, the Union army was not faced with authorized partisan rangers but with guerrilla warfare by unlawful combatants. For example, General Halleck, when in command of the Department of the Missouri, believed that none of the "partisans and guerrilla bands" in the department had been authorized by the Confederate authorities, and directed that both categories of combatants be punished as "mere freebooters and banditti."[12] Based on his experience in the West, when General Grant came East to take command of all the Union armies he initially assumed that Mosby's Rangers were also unlawful combatants: "Where any of Mosby's men are caught," he ordered General Philip Sheridan, "hang them without trial."[13]

Sheridan reported that he had quietly carried out these orders in a few cases, but matters did not come to a head until September 23, 1864, when Union cavalrymen publicly executed six of Mosby's men at Front Royal, Virginia. Another ranger was hanged on October 13.[14] Mosby believed that General George Armstrong Custer's brigade had carried out the executions, and he went through the Confederate chain of command to request authority to retaliate against prisoners from Custer's units. He duly received permission from Richmond to hang seven of Custer's men in retaliation.[15] Seven prisoners of war were chosen by lot for execution. In the end, two escaped and only three were hanged (two more were shot but survived). A placard was placed on one of the bodies announcing that the killings were in retaliation for the Front Royal atrocity. Mosby sent the same message to General Sheridan under a flag of truce. The retaliation appears to have worked, and there were no further executions of Mosby's men.[16]

Retaliation against enemy civilians was instigated principally by acts of unlawful belligerency by civilians, or civilian support for such acts. The customary acts of retaliation included fire, fines, exile, and, in extreme cases, execution of reprisal prisoners. In the summer of 1862, for example, General John Pope, operating in Northern Virginia, issued orders for retaliation against the civilian population for guerrilla attacks on his troops and supply lines:

It is ... ordered that wherever a railroad, wagon road, or telegraph is injured by parties of guerrillas the citizens living within 5 miles of the spot shall be turned out in mass to repair the damage, and shall, beside, pay to the United States in money or in property, to be levied by military force, the full amount of the pay and subsistence of the whole force necessary to coerce the performance of the work during the time occupied in completing it.

If a soldier or legitimate follower of the army be fired upon from any house the house shall be razed to the ground, and the inhabitants sent prisoners to the headquarters of this army. If such an outrage occur at any place distant from settlements, the people within 5 miles around shall be held accountable and made to pay an indemnity sufficient for the case.[17]

As noted in chapter 2, in 1862 Pope had been an informal adviser to President Lincoln, who apparently approved these orders.[18]

Pope's orders gave rise to outrage, particularly in the South and among Northern supporters of his rival, General George McClellan.[19] In reality, however, the terms of this order were not that unusual. Retaliatory burning, fines, and forced labor were widely accepted counter-guerrilla measures. The U.S. Army's 1914 guidance on the law of war stated: "Villages or houses, etc. may be burned for acts of hostility committed from them where the guilty individuals cannot be identified, tried and punished." "Collective punishments," it continued, "may be inflicted either in the form of fine or otherwise," citing with approval the German destruction of a French village and the assessment of a 10 million–franc fine on its inhabitants because they connived with guerrillas during the Franco-Prussian War.[20] During the last phases of the Napoleonic Wars, the Duke of Wellington, commanding British troops in France, threatened to destroy villages and execute reprisal prisoners unless French guerrillas joined the French army and fought as regular soldiers.[21]

John Pope had a reputation for rashness and an "obnoxious personality."[22] It therefore may be appropriate to note that the stolid General George Gordon Meade issued a very similar order a year later in 1863, when guerrilla activity in Northern Virginia again threatened the supply lines of the Army of the Potomac:

> The numerous depredations committed by citizens, or rebel soldiers in disguise, harbored and concealed by citizens, along the Orange and Alexandria Railroad and within our lines, call for prompt and exemplary punishment. Under the instructions of the Government, therefore, every citizen against whom there is sufficient evidence of his having engaged in these practices will be arrested and confined for punishment, or put beyond the lines. The people within 10 miles of the railroad are notified that they will be held responsible in their persons and property for any injury done to the road, trains, depots, or stations by citizens, guerrillas, or persons in disguise; and, in case of such injury, they will be impressed as laborers to repair all damages.[23]

Apparently no houses were actually burned as a result of Pope's 1862 order, but when attacks on the railroad continued in 1863, the U.S. Cavalry under the command of Colonel Charles Russell Lowell was ordered to execute Meade's threat by clearing all inhabitants north of the railroad from Manassas to Alexandria, Virginia, and burning the houses of guerrilla supporters. Lowell made a half-hearted effort to comply, burning two mills and a house and arresting a few adult men who were promptly released.[24]

Retaliatory burning was sometimes carried out far more ruthlessly, however. In the Shenandoah Valley in 1864, General Sheridan reported his response to the apparent assassination of the son of the quartermaster general of the U.S. Army: "Lieut. John R. Meigs, my engineer officer, was murdered beyond Harrisonburg, near Dayton. For this atrocious act all the houses within an area of five miles were burned. Since I came into the Valley, from Harper's Ferry up to Harrisonburg, every [wagon] train, every small party, and every straggler has been bushwhacked by people, many of whom have protection papers from [Union] commanders who have been hitherto in this valley."[25] In his memoirs, Sheridan claimed that the killers had worn Union uniforms and "that the murder had been committed inside our lines was evidence that the perpetrators of the crime, having their homes in the vicinity, had been clandestinely visiting them, and been secretly harbored by some of the neighboring residents."[26] After thirty farm buildings had been burned, Sheridan spared the village of Dayton itself at the urging of one of his officers, whose men had been well treated while stationed near Dayton. The Confederates later claimed that Meigs had been killed by uniformed soldiers in a fair fight; it was raining, and Meigs's killers were wearing ponchos that concealed their Confederate uniforms.[27]

Earlier that summer in the Shenandoah, General David Hunter had burned the home of former governor of Virginia John Letcher in Lexington. Letcher had not personally engaged in hostile acts against Hunter's forces, but Hunter reported he had found in Lexington "a violent and inflammatory proclamation from John Letcher, . . . inciting the population of the country to rise and wage a guerrilla warfare on my troops." Since Letcher himself had fled, Hunter "ordered his property to be burned under my order, published May 24, against persons practicing or abetting such unlawful and uncivilized warfare."[28]

Retaliation in such ambiguous circumstances as the Meigs and Letcher incidents naturally led the other side to assert that these retaliations were not legitimate, and to take counter-retaliatory action of their own. Retaliatory raids could also contribute to the breakdown of military discipline. Soldiers sent to a house or farm thought to be used by guerrillas would often go beyond their orders and pillage the property of owners thought to be disloyal. A Louisiana woman recorded a typical case in her diary:

> Miss Jones, who has just made her escape from town, brings a most dreadful account. She, with seventy-five others, took refuge at Doctor Enders' more than a mile and a half below town. . . . Hearing that guerillas had been there, the Yankees went down, shelled the house in the night, turning all those women and children out, who barely escaped with their clothing, and let the soldiers loose on it. They destroyed everything they could lay their hands on, if it could not be carried off; broke open armoires, trunks, sacked the house, and left it one scene of devastation and ruin. They even stole Miss Jones' braid! She got here with nothing but the clothes she wore.[29]

The Lieber Code counseled retaliation only "after careful inquiry into the real occurrence," and had properly warned that "inconsiderate retaliation removes the belligerents farther and farther from the mitigating rules of regular war, and by rapid steps leads them nearer to the internecine wars of savages."[30] Such escalation is exactly what occurred in the eastern theater of war in the summer of 1864, culminating in the burning of Chambersburg, Pennsylvania, and leading to President Lincoln's call for an agreement for both sides to end house burning.

That an act of retaliation was lawful did not mean that it was wise. Precedents from European wars did not always provide prudent guidance for Union commanders in the Civil War. Wellington and Bismarck could threaten harsh retaliation for the acts of French guerrillas because they knew that their occupation of French soil would eventually end and their soldiers return to England or Prussia. The ultimate goal of the Union army, in contrast, was the reintegration of secessionists into the population of the United States. If they were successful, Pope's, Meade's, and Sheridan's soldiers would end up living as fellow countrymen with the people they tried to control through retaliation. The Lieber Code noted that "in general, military necessity does not include any act of hostility which makes the return to peace unnecessarily difficult."[31] If pressed too vigorously, lawful retaliatory measures could violate this principle.

Nevertheless, retaliation remained a major weapon of Union generals against guerrillas and the civilians who supported them. The forced movement of hostile civilian populations was another common response to guerrilla warfare. The most controversial of General Pope's July 1862 orders called for all adult male civilians in his area of operations to either take an oath of allegiance to the United States or be exiled to Confederate-controlled territory:

> Commanders of army corps, divisions, brigades, and detached commands will proceed immediately to arrest all disloyal male citizens within their lines or within their reach in rear of their respective stations.
>
> Such as are willing to take the oath of allegiance to the United States and will furnish sufficient security for its observance shall be permitted to remain at their homes and pursue in good faith their accustomed avocations. Those who refuse shall be conducted South beyond the extreme pickets of this army.[32]

Pope specifically asked the president for approval of this order, and justified it as necessary to prevent espionage: "I find it impossible to make any movement, however insignificant the force, without having it immediately communicated to the enemy. Constant correspondence, verbally and by letter, between the enemy's forces and the so-called peaceful citizens in the rear of this army, is carried on, which can in no other way be interrupted."[33] We have no record of the president's reply, if any. Pope issued the order the same day he wrote to Lincoln.

In fact, few people were forced into exile under this order.[34] Historian Mark Neely points out that these sweeping calls for mass movement of hostile populations "took place largely only in the realm of ideas."[35] Like Colonel Lowell, ordered to remove the civilians living within ten miles of the Orange and Alexandria railroad, most officers called upon to execute these orders acted feebly, if at all.

There were exceptions. In 1864, General Sherman moved the entire civilian population of Atlanta, Georgia, either to the north or behind Confederate lines. Earlier he had removed all the civilian cotton mill workers in Roswell, Georgia, on the ground that the mills were totally devoted to supporting the Confederate army and that the mill workers were therefore as "subject to the Rules of War" as soldiers in the enemy ranks.[36] Perhaps the most infamous mass removal of civilians occurred in northwestern Missouri in 1863, in what has been called "the harshest act of the U.S. government against its own people in American history."[37] Yet President Lincoln appears to have personally endorsed this order, an act for which he has been roundly criticized.[38]

As the war continued into 1863, guerrilla warfare on the Missouri–Kansas border became increasingly fierce, often breaking down the distinction between civilians and combatants. Although women and children were usually respected, the killing of unarmed men became common. Matters reached a head on August 21, 1863, when Confederate guerrilla leader William Quantrill attacked Lawrence, Kansas, killing 150 men and boys, burning more than 200 buildings, and damaging property to the tune of an estimated $2.5 million.[39]

General Thomas Ewing, commander of the Union Military District of the Border, was away from his Kansas City headquarters at the time of the raid. Concerned that he might be charged with dereliction of duty, and fearing that he had to take strong action against the Missouri guerrillas to prevent retaliatory raids from Kansas irregulars, Ewing issued General Order 11, requiring the depopulation of four counties regarded as guerrilla strongholds:

> All persons living in Jackson, Cass, and Bates Counties, Missouri, and in that part of Vernon included in this district, except those living within ... [a few excepted areas], are hereby ordered to remove from their present places of residence within fifteen days from the date hereof. Those who, within that time, establish their loyalty to the satisfaction of the commanding officer of the military station nearest their present places of residence will receive from him certificates stating the fact of their loyalty, and the names of the witnesses by whom it can be shown. All who receive such certificates will be permitted to remove to any military station in this district, or to any part of the State of Kansas, except the counties on the eastern border of the State. All others shall remove out of this district.[40]

General Order 11 was executed thoroughly and brutally by the Fifteenth Kansas Cavalry, whose troopers held strong feelings against Missourians in general. Around 20,000 people were forced to evacuate and their houses burned. Public outcry in the North was so great that the order was suspended in November.[41]

On September 30, 1863, Lincoln received a delegation of seventy radical Republicans from Missouri who demanded the replacement of General Ewing's immediate superior, General John Schofield, commander of the Department of the Missouri. They accused Schofield of failing to respond vigorously enough to the Lawrence massacre and failing to protect loyal citizens from guerrillas. Lincoln rejected the accusations and refused to relieve General Schofield. He did, however, agree to send Schofield a new set of instructions, which he shared with the radical Missourians. One sentence of the instructions referred to Ewing's mass deportations: "With the matter of removing the inhabitants of certain counties *en masse*; and of removing certain individuals from time to time, who are supposed to be mischievous, I am not now interfering, but am leaving to your own discretion."[42]

Although admirers of Lincoln find this sentence embarrassing, it would have been politically difficult for him to have been openly critical of General Order 11 in this situation. The letter was, after all, written in response to a delegation of Missourians who thought General Schofield was too lenient in his dealing with disloyalty. If the president had criticized him for being too harsh, the disgusted Missourians would undoubtedly have turned to Benjamin Wade, Thaddeus Stevens, and Lincoln's other radical critics in Congress who were more than willing to interfere in his handling of the war. Far from being repealed, General Order 11 might have been written into law and recommended to other generals as an example.

Another difficulty for Lincoln was that Generals Schofield and Ewing could argue with some justification that the order was required by military necessity.[43] In a report to Congress on operations in the western theater, the general in chief of the army, Major General Henry Halleck, justified the order as within the laws and customs of war and required by military necessity, while also noting that the execution of the order had been suspended:

A large part of the military force in the Department of the Missouri has been employed during the past year in repelling raids and in repressing the guerrilla bands of robbers and murderers who have come within our lines or been organized in the country. Most of these bands are not authorized belligerents under the laws of war, but simply outlaws from civilized society. It is exceedingly difficult to eradicate these bands, inasmuch as the inhabitants of the country, sometimes from disloyalty

and sometimes from fear, afford them subsistence and conceal-
ment. . . . In the recent raid of one of these bands into Kansas,
they burned the city of Lawrence and murdered the inhabitants
without regard to age or sex. . . .

These are the terrible results of a border contest, incited at
first for political purposes, and since increased in animosity by
the civil war in which we are engaged, till all sense of humanity
seems to have been lost in the desire to avenge with blood real
or fancied grievances. This extraordinary condition of affairs on
that frontier seems to call for the application of a prompt and
severe remedy.

It has been proposed to depopulate the frontier counties of
Missouri, and to lay waste the country on the border so as to
prevent its furnishing any shelter or subsistence to these bands
of murderers. Such measures are within the recognized laws of
war; they were adopted by Wellington in Portugal, and by the
Russian armies in the campaign of 1812; but they should be
adopted only in case of overruling necessity. The execution of
General Schofield's order on this subject has been suspended,
and it is hoped that it will not be necessary hereafter to renew
it.[44]

As noted earlier, that a military action was legal did not mean it was
prudent under the circumstances. General Order 11 aroused outrage
even in the North. Perhaps the most enduring legacy was a painting by
the pro-Union artist George Caleb Bingham that forcefully depicted
the civilian suffering that General Ewing had caused. President Lincoln
himself regarded forced movement of civilians as a "very strong measure," and was never reluctant to interfere if the military justification
was questionable.[45] He had already taken such action twice in 1863.

In September, the president suspended an order to deport to Confederate territory 400 residents of the Eastern Shore of Virginia who
would not take an oath of allegiance to the Union.[46] There was no clear
military necessity for this act since the Eastern Shore was firmly under
Union control and separated from the rest of Virginia by Chesapeake
Bay. In January, he revoked General Grant's notorious order expelling
"Jews, as a class," from the area of his command, "within twenty four
hours from the receipt of this order by post commanders."[47] Grant was
not generally anti-Semitic, and his biographers have never satisfactorily

explained the reasoning behind the order. He appears to have assumed that Jewish merchants were widely involved in illegal trade with the Confederacy. In any event, there was no military necessity for so sweeping and discriminatory an order, and Lincoln did not hesitate to revoke it.[48]

In Missouri, however, the same could not be said for Ewing's General Order 11. In light of the intractable guerrilla warfare in Missouri, the Lawrence massacre, and the threat of retaliatory atrocities by enraged Kansans, a reasonable case could be made that military necessity required truly drastic action. Nevertheless, when General Schofield read the president's letter, he may not have felt as reassured about General Order 11 as Lincoln's critics have assumed. One student of military history has noted that when dealing with his generals, Lincoln "tended not to order, but to question, prod and suggest."[49] This indirect approach is evident in the president's reference to General Order 11. In the immediately preceding paragraph, Lincoln told Schofield that he "approved" the latter's order imposing martial law, provided "you . . . only arrest individuals, and suppress assemblies, or newspapers, when they may be working *palpable* injury to the military in your charge; and, in no other case . . . interfere with the expression of opinion in any form, or allow it to be interfered with violently by others." Lincoln never told Schofield he "approved" General Order 11, only that he would not interfere with it "now," leaving the issue to the general's "discretion." By itself, this was a rather clear hint that if Schofield's discretion did not lead to mitigation of the order, the commander in chief himself would see it done.

If this hint was not clear enough, at the end of the letter the president gave Schofield specific guidance on several of his responsibilities, including the suppression of guerrilla warfare. "So far as practicable," Lincoln wrote, "you will, by means of your military force, expel guerrillas, marauders, and murderers, and all who are known to harbor, aid, or abet them." There was nothing authorizing the mass expulsion of all the inhabitants of a region. Only those "known" to aid guerrillas—that is, those against whom there was reliable evidence—were to be moved. Either Schofield took these hints himself or someone else did it for him, because within a month Ewing's order was withdrawn.

Aside from the issue of general policy, President Lincoln continued to intervene on behalf of individual Missourians exiled for what appeared to him to be insufficient reason. The case of Dr. Samuel McPheeters, the secessionist Presbyterian minister from St. Louis (discussed in chapter 2), was not the only example.[50] In April 1863, Charles

Drake, the radical leader who later led the Missouri delegation that demanded General Schofield's ouster, wrote the president to protest his lenience toward those exiled for disloyalty:

With the utmost respect, Mr President, I tell you that your tenderness toward rebels and their sympathizers is one of the serious difficulties which the nation has to contend with; and it is particularly felt in Missouri. If the military authorities here were left to deal with rebels as they deserve, and as the officers here, in full view of all the facts, know they deserve, you would have less occasion for anxiety about Missouri; but it is a lamentable fact that as soon as the strong hand falls upon a rebel having friends of high social position, an appeal is made to you by them, and you listen to it, and stop or deaden the descending blow. In nine cases out of ten, the parties who thus successfully invoke your clemency are not Union men at all, however they may represent themselves, or be represented by others; but rebels at heart, who profess Unionism, only because they dare not show their true colors, or, at any rate, sympathizers with the rebellion and with Slavery.[51]

A less serious form of collective punishment than house burning or deportation was assessment of a collective fine or special contribution from the population near the site of a guerrilla raid. As noted earlier, Generals Pope and Meade issued orders holding Virginia civilians financially liable for guerrilla damage to railroads supplying their armies. When a lighthouse was destroyed on the Eastern Shore of Virginia, the local population was suspected of sabotage. A fine of $20,000 was assessed against 221 citizens of Northampton County. President Lincoln suspended payment of the fine, but may have later reinstated it when he learned that local civilians were claiming the suspension was a victory over the federal government.[52] (He later wrote that assessments to pay for guerrilla attacks had had "a very salutary effect" on guerrilla activity "in and about St Louis, and on Eastern Shore of Virginia.")[53] It would be ironic if he did allow the assessment to go forward, since in fact the lighthouse had not been destroyed by local guerrillas but by a Confederate navy raiding party from the Virginia mainland led by Acting Master John Yates Beall.[54] Two years later, Beall's fate would lie in the president's hands (see the conclusion).

Often the funds collected by retaliatory assessments were earmarked to compensate the victims of guerrilla depredations. In Tennessee, when guerrillas killed three captured U.S. soldiers and wounded a fourth, General George Henry Thomas ordered "that the property of . . . rebel citizens living within a circuit of 10 miles of the place where these men were captured be assessed, each in his due proportion according to his wealth, to make up the sum of $30,000, to be divided among the families who were dependent upon the murdered men for support," and that if "the persons assessed fail, within one week after notice shall have been served upon them, to pay in the amount of their tax in money, sufficient of their personal property shall be seized and sold at public auction to make up the amount."[55] When guerrillas killed a steamboat passenger at Rocheport, Missouri, the department commander ordered the townspeople to pay $10,000 for support of the widow and sisters of the deceased, after determining that the local population had "countenanced, tolerated and fed" the attackers.[56]

On the Eastern Shore of Maryland, two churches (presumably with pro-Union congregations) were burnt by parties unknown. General Lew Wallace reacted by ordering the general commanding the district "to ascertain the value of the churches . . . and assess the same upon the disaffected and disloyal citizens in the vicinity of said churches, the money when collected to be handed over to the trustees or other authorized persons of the respective churches."[57]

In Missouri and Kentucky, military commissions or boards were established to assess collective fines against pro-Confederate civilians and distribute the funds to loyal citizens who had suffered property loss at the hands of rebel irregulars. In both states the system became politically controversial.[58] In a sense, military assessments in Maryland, Missouri, and Kentucky were anomalous. In international law, such assessments were proper collective penalties a foreign occupying power imposed on a hostile population. The official view of the Lincoln administration, however, was that these were loyal states and not occupied territory. Such tensions were unavoidable for a government trying to apply international rules to a civil war.

Lincoln was ambivalent about retaliatory assessments. On the one hand, he believed that they deterred guerrilla activity, at least in some circumstances, and he was all for shifting the cost of the war from Northern taxpayers to disloyal citizens. On the other hand, as mentioned earlier, he regarded assessments as a "very strong measure" and was acutely aware of their potential for corruption and unfairness.[59] When Governor Hamilton Gamble of Missouri urged him to suspend the assessment system in that state, the president raised the issue of abuses with General Samuel Curtis, who commanded the Military Department of the Missouri:

> It is urged that . . . assessments are made more for private malice, revenge, and pecuniary interest, than for the public good. This morning I was told by a gentleman who, I have no doubt believes what he says, that in one case of assessments for *ten* thousand dollars, the different persons who paid, compared receipts, and found they had paid *thirty* thousand dollars. If this be true, the inference is that the collecting agents pocketed the odd twenty thousand. And true or not, in the instance, nothing but the sternest necessity can justify the making and maintaining of a system so liable to such abuses. Doubtless the necessity for the making of the system in Missouri *did* exist, and whether it continues for the [maintenance] of it, is now a practical, and very important question.[60]

Curtis responded to the president's concerns rather flippantly:

> Our Union men are much opposed to restraint in their pursuit of rebels, especially in the country where our friends have been persecuted, and where the assessments inure to the benefit of the widows and orphans of men killed by the rebels. There may be frauds, such as you name, but I doubt it. I should have had news of it. No assessment committee could commit such a fraud as you name with impunity.[61]

Lincoln was not impressed, and the general soon received a terse order from the secretary of war to suspend the Missouri assessment system entirely.[62] Curtis was relieved of command later in the year and replaced by General Schofield.

In early 1863, Senator Lazarus Powell of Kentucky complained to the president about the assessment system in his state, asserting that it had been unjustly applied in several cases. Lincoln referred the matter to General Jeremiah T. Boyle, the Union commander in Kentucky, observing that the assessment system, "though just and politic in some cases, is so liable to gross abuse, as to do great injustice in some others and give the government immense trouble."[63] Boyle defended the assessments in question and the president dropped the matter.

When he received another complaint about Kentucky assessments in October 1864, Lincoln's initial reaction was to write a letter defending the system.[64] On reflection, he instead wrote to Major General Stephen Burbridge, General Boyle's successor in the Kentucky command, asking him to comment on the petition and strongly hinting that, as in Missouri, the necessity for such assessments had passed:

> It is represented to me that an officer has, by your authority, assessed and collected considerable sums of money from citizens of Allen and Barren counties, Kentucky, to compensate Union men for depredations committed upon them in the vicinity by rebels; and I am petitioned to order the money to be refunded. At most I could not do this without hearing both sides, which, as yet, I have not. I write now to say, that, in my opinion, in some extreme cases, this class of proceedings becomes a necessity; but that it is liable to—almost inseparable from—great abuses, and therefore should only be sparingly resorted to, and be conducted with great caution; that you, in your department, must be the judge of the proper locations and occasions for applying it; and that it will be well for you to see that your subordinates be at all times ready to account for every dollar, as to why collected, of whom, and how applied. Without this, you will soon find some of them making assessments and collections merely to put money in their own pockets and it will also be impossible to correct errors in future and better times.
>
> In the case I have mentioned, such good men as . . . J. R. Underwood & . . . Henry Grider, though not personally interested, have appealed to me in behalf of others. So soon as you can, consistently with your other duties, I will thank you to acquaint yourself with the particulars of this case, and make any correction which may seem to be proper.[65]

Apparently Burbridge never replied. He probably never had time. Like General Boyle before him, Burbridge and his administration had become intensely controversial in Kentucky, and the general had his hands full answering a variety of charges from his opponents. Within four months, Lincoln would relieve Burbridge at the request of the governor and legislature of Kentucky.[66]

Both Burbridge and Boyle were native Kentuckians, and the president had probably expected that they would be able to successfully navigate the local political waters. As Lowell H. Harrison has noted, however, Kentucky military governors were "in an almost impossible position."[67] From the earliest days of the war, Kentucky had suffered from vicious irregular conflict, particularly in the state's mountainous eastern counties. There, neighbors and prewar friends attacked each other relentlessly, showing little mercy even to sick or unarmed foes.[68] To suppress this seemingly endless violence was the duty of the state's military governors, who also had to implement orders from Washington. In carrying out these duties they would inevitably offend Kentuckians whose activities and property rights were thereby affected. "Just how did one measure civil rights against wartime needs?" Harrison asks.[69] As General Boyle, General Burbridge, and President Lincoln could all testify, there was no ready answer to be found.

General Burbridge issued his most controversial order on July 5, 1864. For every Union man killed by guerrillas, he directed, four captured guerrillas would be shot without trial. Under this order as many as fifty prisoners, including some legitimate prisoners of war, may have been executed.[70]

Retaliatory execution of civilian hostages or prisoners of war, although an extreme measure, was permitted by the laws and usages of war at the time. After World War II, at the principal war crimes trial considering the issue, the court reluctantly concluded that "the practice of killing innocent members of the population as a deterrent to [guerrilla] attacks against . . . troops or acts of sabotage" was still permitted eighty years after the end of the Civil War. "The right to do so has been recognized by many nations including the United States, Great Britain, France and the Soviet Union."[71] The practice was not banned until the adoption of the 1949 Geneva Conventions, which prohibit collective punishment and retaliation against civilians in occupied territory, and the taking of civilian hostages.[72]

Aside from Burbridge's executions, the most notorious killing of reprisal prisoners by the Union occurred, not surprisingly, in Missouri. In 1862, pro-Confederate guerrillas near Palmyra, Missouri, seized Andrew Allsman, a civilian who had assisted Union forces as a guide and informer. To induce his release, General John McNeil announced that he would execute ten captured guerrillas if Allsman was not freed by a certain date. (Since the guerrillas were not regarded as lawful belligerents they were technically civilians.) The deadline passed, and the ten were shot at Palmyra on October 18. The affair became notorious, and Confederate president Jefferson Davis demanded the surrender of McNeil to Confederate authorities for punishment.[73] This was unlikely to happen, but McNeil's supporters in Missouri deluged the White House with petitions that he not be turned over to the Confederates. President Lincoln was at least aware of the incident because he endorsed the envelope containing the petitions.[74] Lincoln may have done nothing in McNeil's case because the damage had already been done, and there seemed to be widespread support for his act as a legitimate response to unlawful guerrilla actions.

Lincoln himself signed one order for retaliation against Confederate prisoners of war. In response to Confederate threats to enslave African American U.S. soldiers and execute their officers for inciting slave rebellion,[75] on July 30, 1863, the president signed an Order of Retaliation intended to deter the implementation of these threats:

> It is the duty of every Government to give protection to its citizens, of whatsoever class, color, or condition, and especially to those who are duly organized as soldiers in the public service. The law of nations and the usages and customs of war, as carried on by civilized powers, permit no distinction as to color in the treatment of prisoners of war as public enemies. To sell or enslave any captured person on account of his color and for no offense against the laws of war is a relapse into barbarism and a crime against the civilization of the age.
>
> The Government of the United States will give the same protection to all its soldiers; and if the enemy shall sell or enslave any one because of his color, the offense shall be punished by retaliation upon the enemy's prisoners in our possession.
>
> It is therefore ordered that for every soldier of the United States killed in violation of the laws of war, a rebel soldier shall be executed; and for every one enslaved by the enemy or sold into slavery, a rebel soldier shall be placed at hard labor on the public works.[76]

That the president never implemented this order suggests the distaste Lincoln felt for actually ordering the innocent to suffer for offenses they had not committed. Similarly, after the massacre of African American soldiers at Fort Pillow on April 17, 1864, the attorney general advised the president that retaliation was legally permissible, and the secretary of war advised selecting by lot Confederate officers for retaliation from among those held as prisoners of war, but Lincoln never followed through.[77] A partially completed draft order to Stanton appears among Lincoln's published papers, but it was never sent.[78]

The great African American abolitionist Frederick Douglass recalled the president's emotional response when Douglass urged him to retaliate against Confederate prisoners of war for the killing of African American soldiers: "I shall never forget the benignant expression of his face, the tearful look of his eye and the quiver in his voice, when he deprecated a resort to retaliatory measures. 'Once begun,' he said, 'I do not know where such a measure would stop.' He said he could not take men out and kill them in cold blood for what was done by others. If he could get hold of the persons who were guilty of killing the colored prisoners in cold blood, the case would be different, but he could not kill the innocent for the guilty."[79] The same reluctance to punish the innocent is evident in the president's handling of petitions on behalf of individual prisoners selected for retaliation by commanders in the field. He saved from execution at least one of Burbridge's retaliation prisoners, "an inexperienced boy named W E Walker," when a former Union cavalry officer brought the case to his attention.[80]

In November 1864, several prominent Missourians asked the president to intervene in the case of Enoch O. Wolf, who was to be executed in retaliation for the killing of Major James Wilson after he had been captured by guerrillas.[81] Lincoln telegraphed General William Rosecrans, who then had the misfortune to command the Department of the Missouri, to suspend the execution and report the facts of the case to him.[82] General Rosecrans pushed back hard, arguing that this retaliatory execution was necessary to the security of his men:

In compliance with your telegraphic orders of the 10th inst[tant] I transmit . . . a printed statement of the case of Major Wolf, C. S. A. and of the other rebels who were executed by my orders, for the purpose of teaching the enemy that if the laws of war and humanity are not sufficient to secure our prisoners from murder, I will add to their force the motive of personal interest.

Your Excellency will perceive a case of cold blooded murder of Major Wilson, and five other prisoners of war by the permission, or orders, of Confederate Officers, as well proven as the mind of any intelligent man could require.

As to the rights and even duty of a Commander to hold the members of any organized body of men responsible for the actions of their organization, I presume there can be no doubt. War itself proceeds on this ground to kill men who individually have done no wrong, and to destroy the property of those who individually have not harmed the Nation who makes it.

As to the policy of doing as I have done I leave you to judge after reading the records in this case. All other motive having failed to secure my soldiers who have surrendered themselves prisoners of war from cold blooded assassination or official murder by [Confederate general Sterling] Price's Command, I felt bound to appeal to the sense of personal security by declaring to these men that I should hold them individually responsible for the treatment of my Troops while prisoners in their hands.[83]

The president knew General Rosecrans as a talented but badly flawed officer. Rosecrans was not without abilities. In 1842 he had graduated from West Point fifth out of a class of fifty-six cadets. After leaving the army in 1854, he became a successful engineer and businessman. Early in the Civil War, he drove Confederate forces from Northwestern Virginia, an accomplishment for which his superior, General McClellan, successfully claimed the credit in Washington. At the beginning of 1863, General Rosecrans earned President Lincoln's gratitude as commander of the Army of the Cumberland. After the abject defeat of the Army of the Potomac at Fredericksburg in December 1862, Rosecrans's victory over General Braxton Bragg at the battle of Murfreesboro, or Stones River, on January 2, 1863, raised Union morale and took pressure off the president to withdraw his Emancipation Proclamation. "God bless you, and all with you," Lincoln wired Rosecrans on January 5.[84]

However, the president began to develop doubts about Rosecrans's judgment after he failed to follow up Murfreesboro by pursuing and attacking Bragg's army. Like many West Point graduates, Rosecrans was a follower of the Swiss military theorist Antoine Jomini, who emphasized capture of strategic areas of land by maneuver rather than defeating the enemy in battle.[85] Lincoln, in contrast, had come to believe that the key to victory was the capture or destruction of Confederate armies rather than occupying enemy cities and territory. As he would later write to General Joseph Hooker, "I think *Lee's* army, and not *Richmond,* is your true objective point."[86] For his part, Rosecrans could never understand why the president did not appreciate the bloodless victory he achieved by maneuvering Bragg to abandon Chattanooga, Tennessee, on September 8, 1863.

On September 20, however, Bragg defeated Rosecrans's Army of the Cumberland at the battle of Chickamauga. During the battle, General Rosecrans apparently panicked and fled back to Chattanooga, where his army was besieged by Bragg until rescued by forces under General Grant. Assistant Secretary of War Charles Dana, who was traveling with Grant, reported to the White House that Rosecrans was "for the present completely broken down." President Lincoln remarked that since his defeat at Chickamauga, Rosecrans seemed "confused and stunned like a duck hit on the head."[87] Relieved by Grant at Chattanooga, Rosecrans was placed in command of the Department of the Missouri in early 1864. Mark Neely has noted that by this time in the Civil War, the Missouri command had become a kind of exile for defeated Union officers. "Generals were transferred to Missouri if they failed at the war's important tasks."[88]

Recognizing the difficult situation Rosecrans faced, and still grateful for the victory at Murfreesboro, on this occasion Lincoln decided to defer to Rosecrans's judgment, while also issuing an important warning: "A Major Wolf, as it seems, was under sentence, in your Department, to be executed in retaliation for the murder of a Major Wilson; and I, without any particular knowledge of the facts, was induced, by appeals for mercy, to order the suspension of his execution until further order. Understanding that you so desire, this letter places the case again within your control, with the remark only that I wish you to do nothing merely for revenge, but that what you may do, shall be solely done with reference to the security of the future."[89]

Although, as Frederick Douglass recorded, Lincoln would not himself order retaliatory killing in cold blood for what was done by others, he would defer to his commanders in the field in extreme cases. However, he once again pushed home the point that killing in war could be justified only if it pursued rational military goals, and not merely emotional satisfaction of revenge.

Upon reflection, General Rosecrans decided that perhaps the execution of Wolf was not really necessary; six other prisoners had already been executed in retaliation for the six Union soldiers executed along with Major Wilson. Major Wolf survived and was exchanged for a Confederate prisoner of war in February 1865.

4

"War, at the Best, Is Terrible"

Devastation and Command Responsibility

In defense of the order authorizing his soldiers to live off the land, General John Pope's official report on his 1862 campaign in Virginia asserted that orders to subsist off the country were "common in the history of warfare" and that his orders were "well calculated to secure efficient and rapid operations of the army, and, in case of reverse, to leave the enemy without the means of subsisting in the country over which our army had passed, and over which any pursuit must be conducted." Although General Robert E. Lee defeated Pope's army at the Second Battle of Bull Run and forced it back into the defenses of Washington, General Pope argued that the "long delay and embarrassment of the army under General Lee, in its subsequent movements toward Washington, occasioned largely by the want of supplies taken from the country under this order, fully justified its wisdom."[1]

Laying waste to the countryside to impair an enemy's advance was a common and accepted practice in European warfare.[2] There were even technical military terms to refer to the practice—"devastation," "ravaging," or "desolating" a territory. The Swiss legal writer Emmerich de Vattel distinguished "wasting" a country of military supplies from the more severe act of "ravaging" it, and reasoned that both could be lawful acts of war depending on circumstances:

If it is lawful to take away the property of an unjust enemy in order to weaken or punish him, the same motives justify us in destroying what we cannot conveniently carry away. Thus, we waste a country, and destroy the provisions and forage, that the enemy may not find a subsistence there. . . .

On certain occasions, however, matters are carried still farther: a country is totally ravaged, towns and villages are sacked,
and delivered up a prey to fire and sword. . . . We ravage a
country and render it uninhabitable, in order to make it serve
us as a barrier, and to cover our frontier against an enemy whose
incursions we are unable to check by any other means. A cruel
expedient, it is true: but why should we not be allowed to adopt
it at the expense of the enemy, since, with the same view, we
readily submit to lay waste our own provinces?[3]

Very early in the Civil War the Confederacy adopted a policy to "lay
waste" a part of its territory in the face of a Federal invasion. In June
1861, Confederate military authorities ordered General Joseph Johnston, then commanding Confederate forces in Northern Virginia, to
"seek to strip [the] country which may be possessed by the enemy of
those things which may be most available to him, especially horses suit-
ed to the military service and herds of beef cattle."[4]

It is worth noting that, at the time of the Civil War, army commanders had no recognized obligation to ensure that enemy civilians
did not starve. Indeed, the Lieber Code flatly stated: "It is lawful to
starve the hostile belligerent, armed or unarmed, so that it leads to the
speedier subjection of the enemy."[5] It was not until 1949 that the duty
of ensuring civilians were adequately fed was imposed on occupying
armies.[6] Starvation of civilians as a method of warfare was not formally
prohibited until 1977.[7]

In December 1863, when Confederate raiders destroyed General
Ulysses S. Grant's supply depot at Holly Springs, Mississippi, Grant
recalled that local citizens approached him "with broad smiles on their
faces indicating intense joy, to ask what I was going to do now without anything for my soldiers to eat." When he told them he had sent
troops and wagons to collect food in the countryside, their expressions
changed, and they asked, "What are *we* to do?" Grant remembered:
"My response was that we had endeavored to feed ourselves from our
own northern resources while visiting them; but their friends in gray
had been uncivil enough to destroy what we had brought along, and it
could not be expected that men, with arms in their hands, would starve
in the midst of plenty. I advised them to emigrate east, or west, fifteen
miles and assist in eating up what we left."[8]

In practice, this strict policy was applied only when the Union forces were temporarily in hostile territory. Once the U.S. Army established stable control over an area, it usually ended up feeding the local population, whatever their political loyalties.[9] Even Grant ordered his foragers to leave two months' food supplies for the Mississippians whose stores were taken by his foragers. Still, Union soldiers and Southern civilians might have very different concepts of the amount of food necessary to survive for two months. In July 1864, one Mississippi farm wife, Elizabeth Beach, complained that Union foragers had left her and her husband, Asa, little or nothing to eat: "They left me nothing to eat at all. Took *every solitary* thing I had, except one jar of lard and my salt. There was not even a grain of corn on the place to make hominy after they were gone and we had enough of every thing to last us until christmas. I hated their taking my chickens and groceries worse than any thing else."[10] Mrs. Beach also found, however, that humanitarian appeals could sometimes be effective even with foragers: "They killed all of Asa's hogs for next years meat but we happened to save our cows. They killed nearly everybody's cows and calves around here but ours. . . . They started to shoot them several times, but I ran after them and begged them not to kill them. Told them they had taken everything I had to eat, but if they would leave the calves that we could live on milk and bread."[11]

Even under the lax standards of the past, it was possible to go too far in ravaging an enemy's territory. In the late 1600s, the devastation of the Rhineland area of Germany, which included destruction of the city of Heidelberg, by the armies of Louis XIV of France was denounced throughout Europe as excessive.[12] Still, the basic legitimacy of desolating a land to impede the enemy was reaffirmed as recently as 1948. During the final days of World War II, General Lothar Rendulic commanded German forces occupying the Norwegian province of Finnmark, on the border of the Soviet Union. Believing he was about to be attacked by the Soviets he devastated the area through which the Red Army would most likely pass, razing almost every building after removing the Norwegian civilian population. In fact, the Soviets never attacked his forces. Following the war, he was charged before an Allied military tribunal with the war crime of destroying civilian property without military necessity. The court concluded that based on the facts known to him at the time, General Rendulic honestly believed that the devastation was a military necessity, and found him not guilty of this charge.[13]

Did President Lincoln believe that devastation of an area was one of the "other military purposes" for which civilian property could legitimately be destroyed under his order of July 22, 1862?[14] The evidence is ambiguous.

During the summer of 1864, while Grant was besieging Lee's army at Petersburg, General Lee dispatched a full army corps under General Jubal Early to the Shenandoah Valley to throw back an invading Union force under General David Hunter and, once this was accomplished, to attack Washington, D.C. Even a brief Confederate occupation of the U.S. capital would have a disastrous effect on Northern morale, and might even encourage European powers to consider recognition of the Confederacy. Quickly pushing Hunter's force into the mountains of West Virginia, Early crossed the Potomac on July 5. By July 11, Early's army was on the outskirts of Washington. Only the arrival of reinforcements from the Army of the Potomac led him to retreat back to the Shenandoah.

The security of the federal capital was a primary concern of President Lincoln's throughout the war, and Early's nearly successful attack was a major embarrassment for General Grant. To prevent Early from trying a repeat performance, Grant ordered General Hunter to devastate the lower Shenandoah Valley. On July 17, Army Chief of Staff Henry Halleck informed Hunter:

> General Grant has directed . . . that, with the troops belonging to your command, you pursue the enemy cautiously . . . if you can. He further directs that "if compelled to fall back you will retreat in front of the enemy toward the main crossings of the Potomac, so as to cover Washington, and not be squeezed out to one side, so as to make it necessary to fall back into West Virginia to save your army." "If Hunter cannot get to Gordonsville and Charlottesville to cut the railroads he should make all the valleys south of the Baltimore and Ohio road a desert as high up as possible. I do not mean that houses should be burned, but every particle of provisions and stock should be removed, and the people notified to move out." He further says "that he wants your troops to eat out Virginia clear and clean as far as they go, so that crows flying over it for the balance of the season will have to carry their provender with them."[15]

This was a classic military use of devastation—to impede the movement of a hostile army through a specific route.[16] President Lincoln probably knew about this order. From 1861 onward, he routinely monitored military telegraph traffic between the War Department and the field.[17] He would have relied on telegraph monitoring even more in 1864–1865, because General Grant was not personally present in Washington, having established his headquarters at City Point, Virginia, during the siege of Petersburg. On more than one occasion in the summer of 1864 the president personally intervened in military telegraphic exchanges between Grant and his subordinates.[18]

If rigorously executed, Grant's order would bring economic disaster to hundreds of families in the Shenandoah Valley. (Although Grant made it clear that dwelling houses should not be burned, throughout the Civil War owners who left their homes unoccupied often returned to find the houses had been burned by soldiers regardless of official orders.) There were, however, sound military reasons for such an extreme measure, since for three years the valley had annually served as an invasion route for Confederate forces. Clearly it was not just an act of revenge or malice. If he knew about Grant's order, the president did not intervene.

From William Tecumseh Sherman and George Armstrong Custer in the North to Stonewall Jackson and J. E. B. Stuart in the South, Civil War armies were often led by some very odd characters. Even for a Civil War general, however, David Hunter was exceptionally moody and emotional. In July 1864, having been soundly defeated by Jubal Early and believing that the government blamed him for Early's attack on Washington, General Hunter was entering what a sympathetic biographer termed "a particularly dark period, ordering many actions that were certainly beyond normal military practice."[19] Rather than implement Grant's order, Hunter began a series of actions that went far beyond what the general in chief had directed.

Although Grant had stated he did not want houses burned, on July 17, Hunter ordered Captain F. G. Martindale, First New York Cavalry, to "burn the dwelling-house and outbuildings of Andrew Hunter," at Charlestown, West Virginia, and then proceed to Martinsburg, West Virginia, to "burn the dwelling-house and outbuildings of Charles J. Faulkner." Andrew Hunter had been a Virginia state senator in the secessionist government; Charles Faulkner had served on the staff of Stonewall Jackson and was suspected of other aid to the enemy. In both cases, Captain Martindale was ordered not to permit any furniture or other personal property to be taken from the houses.[20] These orders were apparently issued in retaliation for the burning of the Maryland governor's house by Early's forces, which the Confederates justified as retaliation for the burning of former Virginia governor John Letcher's house by Hunter.[21]

In accordance with his orders, Captain Martindale arrested Andrew Hunter and burned his house. Charles Faulkner was not at home when Martindale's soldiers arrived, but his wife, Mary Boyd Faulkner, quickly got in touch with a friendly Union officer who contacted President Lincoln. The president cut the chain of command and telegraphed Captain Martindale directly: "The property of Charles J. Faulkner is exempt from the order of General David S. Hunter, for the burning of the residences of prominent citizens of the Shenandoah Valley in retaliation for the burning of Governor Bradford's house in Maryland by the Confederate forces."[22] Although Grant's order had an apparent military justification, it was just as clear that Hunter's order was punitive in intent. The injunction to prevent the inhabitants from removing personal property before their houses were demolished could be intended only to increase their suffering at the loss of prized possessions. This order was too close to destruction for wantonness and revenge for Lincoln's comfort.

Hunter's order did not give any reason for the destruction; the speculation that it was in retaliation for the burning of Governor Augustus Bradford's house must have been included in Mrs. Faulkner's appeal to the president. It has been argued that from the wording of his message, it was "obvious that Lincoln knew of Hunter's orders and did not disapprove or he would have stopped any further destruction and arrests."[23] However, General Hunter's order directed Captain Martindale to burn Andrew Hunter's house before Faulkner's. By the time Mrs. Faulkner approached Lincoln, it would have been too late to save the first house. In any event, the pattern of presidential behavior is familiar—intervening in a specific case where military authority was abused, but offering no general directions to prevent future abuses.

In separate orders, Hunter had directed the destruction of two more houses, but there is no evidence that these actions were ever brought to the president's attention. One of the houses to be burned was Bedford, the home of Mrs. Henrietta Lee, whose husband was a distant relative of Robert E. Lee. Articulate and highly literate, Mrs. Lee wrote General Hunter a letter that has become a classic expression of Southern outrage over the military destruction of private property for no discernable military reason:

General Hunter—Yesterday your underling, Captain Martindale, of the first New York Cavalry, executed your infamous order and burned my house. You have the satisfaction 'ere this of receiving from him the information that your orders were fulfilled to the letter; the dwelling and other outbuildings, seven in number, with their contents, being burned, I, therefore, a helpless woman whom you have cruelly wronged, address you, a major-general of the United States Army, and demand why this was done? What was my offense?

My husband was absent—an exile. He had never been a politician or in any way engaged in the struggle now going on, his age preventing. This fact your chief of staff, David Strother, could have told you. The house was built by my father, a Revolutionary soldier, who served the whole seven years for your independence. There was I born; there the sacred dead repose. It was my home and there has your niece (Miss Griffith) who has tarried among us all in this horrid war up to the present moment, met with all kindness and hospitality at my hands. Was it for this you turned me, my young daughter, and little son out upon the world without a shelter?

Or was it because my husband is the grandson of the Revolutionary patriot and "rebel," Richard Henry Lee, and the near kinsman of the noblest of Christian warriors, the greatest of generals, Robert E. Lee? Heaven's blessings be upon his head forever! You and your government have failed to conquer, subdue or match him; and disappointed rage and malice find vent on the helpless and inoffensive. Hyena-like you have torn my heart to pieces, for all hallowed memories clustered around that homestead; and demon-like you have done it without even the pretext of revenge, for I never saw or harmed you. Your office is not to lead like a brave man and soldier your men to fight in the ranks of war, but your work has been to separate yourself from all danger, and with your incendiary band steal unawares upon helpless women and children to insult and destroy. Two fair homes did you yesterday ruthlessly lay in ashes, giving not a moment's warning to the startled inmates of your wicked purpose; turning mothers and children out of doors, your very name is execrated by your own men for the cruel work you give them to do.

In the case of Mr. A. R. Boteler, both father and mother were far away. Any heart but that of Captain Martindale (and yours) would have been touched by that little circle, comprising a widowed daughter just risen from her bed of illness, her three fatherless babies—the eldest five years old—and her heroic sister. I repeat, any man would have been touched at the sight but Captain Martindale! One might as well hope to find mercy and feeling in the heart of a wolf bent on his prey of young lambs, as to search for such qualities in his bosom. You have chosen well your agent for such deeds, and doubtless will promote him.

A colonel of the Federal Army has stated that you deprived forty of your officers of their commands because they refused to carry out your malignant mischief. All honor to their names for this, at least! They are men, and have human hearts and blush for such a commander! I ask who that does not wish infamy and disgrace attached to him forever would serve under you? Your name will stand on history's pages as the Hunter of weak women, and innocent children; the Hunter to destroy defenseless villages and beautiful homes—to torture afresh the agonized hearts of widows; the Hunter of Africa's poor sons and daughters, to lure them on to ruin and death of soul and body; the Hunter with the relentless heart of a wild beast, the face of a fiend, and the form of a man. Oh, Earth! Behold the monster! Can I say "God forgive you"? No prayer can be offered for you! Were it possible for human lips to raise your name heavenward, angels would thrust the foul thing back again, and demons claim their own. The curse of thousands, the scorn of the manly and upright, and the hatred of the true and honorable, will follow you and yours through all time, and brand your name infamy! Infamy!

Again, I demand why have you burned my house? Answer as you must answer before the Searcher of all hearts; why have you added this cruel, wicked deed to your many crimes?[24]

The Lieber Code should have warned General Hunter that the law of war did not sanction acts of pure revenge and that "military necessity [did] not include any act of hostility which makes the return to peace unnecessarily difficult."[25] The anger expressed in Mrs. Lee's letter sadly illustrates how wanton destruction could create major barriers to the return of peace, particularly in a civil war.

General Hunter next went beyond unauthorized house burning. Relying on Grant's order to remove the population of the lower Shenandoah Valley, General Hunter ordered that the disloyal inhabitants of Frederick, Maryland, who had informed on their Unionist neighbors during General Early's occupation, be taken into custody. The men were to be imprisoned in Wheeling, West Virginia, and the women and children banished to areas under Confederate control.[26] Of course, Frederick, Maryland, was not part of the Shenandoah Valley of Virginia, the subject of Grant's order. This directive went so far beyond Grant's order that even the tough-minded Secretary of War Edwin Stanton thought it odd and brought it to the president's attention. (Perhaps Stanton became more sensitive to the president's humanitarian interests after he had found himself at cross-purposes with Lincoln over military control of churches.) Lincoln promptly ordered Stanton to "suspend the order of Gen. Hunter" until further notice and "direct him to send to the Department, a brief report of what is known against" each person to be taken into custody.[27] A report would allow Stanton and the president to assess whether there was any legitimate security requirement for the arrests. Four days later, Hunter surrendered command in the Shenandoah to General Philip Sheridan, who was more interested in engaging Early's army than arresting disloyal Maryland citizens. The whole matter appears to have been dropped.

In the meantime, General Grant began to focus attention on destroying Jubal Early's army rather than creating a barrier to future invasions. Placing the trusted Sheridan in command was part of this process, but Grant also reassessed his initial order to depopulate the lower Shenandoah Valley. On August 5, he signed orders to Hunter, later handed on to Sheridan, advising that during his advance up the Shenandoah, it was desirable that "nothing should be left to invite the enemy to return"; but the idea of forcing the inhabitants into exile had been conspicuously dropped. Instead, General Hunter should try to persuade the population that it was not in their economic interest for Early's army to return: "Take all provisions, forage, and stock wanted for the use of your command; such as cannot be consumed, destroy. It is not desirable that the buildings should be destroyed; they should rather be protected; but the people should be informed that so long as an army can subsist among them recurrences of these raids must be expected, and we are determined to stop them at all hazards. . . . . Make your own arrangements for supplies of all kinds, giving regular vouchers for such as will be taken from loyal citizens in the country through which you march."[28] Perhaps someone had brought to Grant's attention the president's orders of July 22, 1862, on the treatment of enemy property. His new emphasis on giving "regular vouchers" for supplies would have complied with Lincoln's order that "accounts shall be kept sufficiently accurate and in detail to show quantities and amounts and from whom" property was requisitioned.[29]

On occasion, Grant still referred to making the Shenandoah Valley a "barren waste," but the meaning of that phrase had altered considerably since July. The emphasis now was on damaging railroads and crops and carrying off stock.[30] Sheridan had an opportunity to execute Grant's program of destruction after defeating General Early at the battles of Opequon (Third Winchester), on September 19, and Fisher's Hill, on September 21 and 22, 1864. Making his headquarters at the town of Harrisonburg, he sent three cavalry divisions to destroy railroads, mills, barns, food, and forage from September 25 to October 8.[31] To Grant's prohibition on destroying private homes, he added protection for the farms of widows.

Needless to say, General Philip Sheridan is not a popular historical figure among descendants of the valley's Civil War inhabitants. Nevertheless, one student of the campaign, who has collected family traditions from these descendants, has found evidence that Union cavalrymen generally tried to respect these restrictions.[32] Ironically, one widow whose property suffered despite Sheridan's orders was Mary Homan Lincoln. Her husband, Colonel Abraham Lincoln, had been first cousin to the president's father, Thomas Lincoln. As John Heatwole notes, "On the farm where the President's father had been born eighty-six years earlier, Union troopers burned the barn, corncrib and carriage house." They also reported destroying 350 bushels of wheat and seventeen tons of hay and straw. Heatwole skeptically observes that "if the barn actually held that much fodder, it must have been a tremendous fire."[33]

Rather than driving the inhabitants south into Confederate territory, Sheridan offered transportation north for any who wanted to leave. About 400 Dunkers, a pacifist sect who, Sheridan reported, had suffered under Confederate draft laws, took advantage of this offer.[34] (In presenting himself to Grant as a champion of the Dunkers, Sheridan was more than a little disingenuous. Dunkers had owned many of the thirty or so farm buildings he ordered burned in retaliation for the killing of Lieutenant John Meigs.)

Recent studies have argued that Sheridan's memoirs exaggerated the scale of destruction his men achieved and its impact on the siege of Richmond, and that earlier historians erroneously took these claims at face value. Either most of the food and forage in the valley had already been exhausted, it is argued, or the time and resources Sheridan devoted to their destruction were so limited that the impact was uneven at best.[35]

The field reports of Sheridan and his subordinates lend some support to both of these revisionist views. When he was in the area of New Market, Sheridan reported to Grant that he was having difficulty supplying his army because there were "not sufficient [supplies] in the Valley to live off the country."[36] When he reached Harrisonburg, he similarly reported that he could not send his infantry over the Blue Ridge Mountains to tear up the Virginia Central railroad because he could not "accumulate sufficient stores." Nevertheless, in the same report he claimed that "the destruction of the grain and forage from here to Staunton will be a terrible blow" to the Confederacy.[37] Grain and forage in the vicinity of Staunton was, he reported, kept in the valley for the use of Early's army, while farther south the "grain and forage from Staunton up to Lexington had [already] been sent to Richmond."[38]

Since the supplies for Richmond were already gone, Sheridan's "terrible blow" would land not on the defenders of the Confederate capital, but rather on what was left of Early's army after its recent defeats. Sheridan's division commanders reported impressive quantities of supplies destroyed (e.g., 10,000 bushels of wheat for the Third Cavalry Division and an astounding 410,742 bushels for the First Cavalry Division).[39] However, the report of General William Powell, commanding the Second Cavalry Division, casts doubt on the thoroughness of the operation. Rather than listing in detail property destroyed, as had the other division commanders, Powell simply estimated that the total "grain, forage, flouring mills, tanneries, blast furnaces, &c. [destroyed], and stock driven off" by the Second Division was worth at least $3 million. He then casually added that despite this destruction, there was "still considerable forage and stock in the valley, east of the Blue Ridge, [and] adjacent to the headwaters of the Rappahannock."[40]

In terms of Emmerich de Vattel's distinction between committing "waste" on an enemy's land and the more brutal "ravaging" of it,

Sheridan's 1864 campaign fits the former category more neatly than the latter.[41] In the end, Sheridan did little in the Shenandoah Valley that went beyond President Lincoln's orders on enemy property issued two years earlier.

For most people, the terms "devastation" and "Civil War" bring to mind General William Tecumseh Sherman's march through Georgia and the Carolinas in 1864–1865. Sherman was different from Sheridan, both in his policies and in the military situation he faced.

For two centuries, professional military officers in Europe and America usually tried to prevent their soldiers from pillaging and looting civilian property. Their concerns were not humanitarian so much as disciplinary. Soldiers engaged in looting, rape, and other abuses of the civilian population were no longer under the control of their officers, and the dissolute habits acquired in the course of these activities might lead to disobedience in battle.[42] Sherman, a West Point graduate, fully shared these professional attitudes. Early in the Civil War he had futilely tried to impose regular army discipline on his individualistic volunteer soldiers. "I would not let our men burn fence rails for fire or gather fruit or vegetable though hungry, and these were the property of outspoken rebels," he later wrote. "We at that time were restrained, tied by a deep-seated reverence for law and property."[43]

In July 1862, President Lincoln authorized Union armies to live off the land, and in December of that year, General Grant, Sherman's commander, discovered that this was a practical alternative to maintaining lengthy lines of supply subject to disruption by Confederate raiders. Building on this knowledge, Sherman concluded that the occasional irrepressible lawlessness of his soldiers could produce military and political benefits.

In 1863, following the surrender of Vicksburg, Grant assigned Sherman the task of repelling the Confederate army that General Joe Johnston had gathered to try to relieve the siege of that city. In the face of Sherman's advance, Johnston devastated central Mississippi to slow or impede his adversary. Kerosene was dumped into cisterns, and rotting animal corpses left in other water sources.[44] The Federal army suffered, and replied in kind. In July, Sherman reported to Grant:

> We are absolutely stripping the country of corn, cattle, hogs, sheep, poultry, everything, and the new-growing corn is being thrown open as pasture fields or hauled for the use of our ani-

mals. The wholesale destruction to which this country is now being subjected is terrible to contemplate, but it is the scourge of war, to which ambitious men have appealed, rather than the judgment of the learned and pure tribunals which our forefathers had provided for supposed wrongs and injuries. Therefore, so much of my instructions [from Grant] as contemplated destroying and weakening the resources of our enemy are being executed with rigor, and we have also done much toward the destruction of Johnston's army.[45]

Johnston was forced to retreat, and Sherman learned lessons in Mississippi that he would later apply in Georgia and the Carolinas, both on the utility of an army living off the countryside and on its psychological impact on the hostile civilian population.

Sherman, highly familiar with, and even sympathetic to, the Southern way of life, had speculated to Grant on the impact on Confederate morale of Union armies living off their lands. "They cannot be made to love us," he wrote to his friend and superior, "but may be made to fear us, and dread the passage of troops through their country." "We cannot change the hearts of those people of the South," he continued "but we can make war so terrible that they will realize the fact that, however brave and gallant and devoted to their country, still they are mortal and should exhaust all peaceful remedies before they fly to war."[46]

Sherman's experiences while pursuing Joe Johnson confirmed these conclusions and suggested that, if Southern hearts could not be changed, threats to Southern property could change Southern political calculations:

Judge Sharkey, Dr. Poindexter, and Mr. Yerger, with many other very intelligent and influential men [in Mississippi], have consulted me as to moving in the matter of organizing the State to submit to the lawful authority of the United States. They admit themselves beaten, subdued, and charge their rulers and agitators with bringing ruin and misery on the State. Of course, I make no promises or pledges, but merely state that I believe such a movement would be received with favor. . . .

I profess to know nothing of politics, but I think we have here an admirable wedge which may be encouraged without committing the President or War Department. If prominent men in Mississippi admit the fact of being subdued, it will have a powerful effect all over the South.[47]

Obsession with property was the Achilles' heel of the Confederacy. "For all the proclamations about states' rights and the preservation of liberty as envisioned by the Founding Fathers," one student of Sherman has noted, "for all the shrill posturing about a distinctively Southern culture, Sherman had a keen appreciation that the landed wealthy had championed secession mostly for the preservation and expansion of their own vast estates and black Helots—property, not ideas, was the issue."[48] A Confederate government that could not protect its citizens' property would lose legitimacy.

A little over a year later, Sherman captured Atlanta, Georgia. On September 7, the day he entered the city, he announced plans to turn Atlanta into a fortified military stronghold. Not wanting to control and feed a hostile population in a Union fortress, he expelled the entire civilian population from Atlanta, offering them a choice of transportation, with their personal property, north to Tennessee or Kentucky, or south to the Confederate lines controlled by General John Bell Hood.[49]

The decision led to a sharp exchange of letters between Sherman, Hood, and the city authorities of Atlanta, in which Sherman stoutly defended his act as within the existing laws and customs of war, citing parallel actions on the Confederate side.[50] This correspondence also produced some of Sherman's most notable quotations, including "War is cruelty and you cannot refine it," and "You might as well appeal against the thunder storm as against these terrible hardships of war." Still, when Sherman published his memoirs years later, at the end of this correspondence he proudly included a letter from Army Chief of Staff Henry Halleck, approving the removal of civilians from Atlanta: "The course which you have pursued in removing rebel families from Atlanta, . . . is fully approved by the War Department. Not only are you justified by the laws and usages of war in removing these people, but I think it was your duty to your own army to do so."[51] Although General Halleck has gone down in history as a poor military leader, in the nineteenth century he was an authority on international law, having produced a multivolume treatise on the subject. Sherman undoubtedly saw this dispatch as a vindication of his Atlanta policy.[52]

By October, Sherman was having serious doubts about operating from Atlanta. His base there was dependent for supplies on a single rail line more than a hundred miles long, extending back to Chattanooga, Tennessee. General Hood's Confederates could continually cut it, forcing Sherman to protect his rear rather than go on the offensive. His solution was the famous "march to the sea." He would cut his army loose from Atlanta and the Chattanooga rail line and move cross-country to the Atlantic coast, living off the land. On October 11, he tested the idea on General Grant:

> I would infinitely prefer to make a wreck of the road and of the country from Chattanooga to Atlanta, including the latter city, send back all my wounded and worthless [troops], and, with my effective army, move through Georgia, smashing things to the sea. Hood may turn into Tennessee and Kentucky, but I believe he will be forced to follow me. Instead of being on the defensive, I would be on the offensive; instead of guessing at what he means to do, he would have to guess at my plans. . . . I can make Savannah [Georgia], Charleston [South Carolina], or the mouth of the Chattahoochee [on the Gulf coast].[53]

President Lincoln expressed doubts about Sherman's proposal, concerned that "a misstep by General Sherman might be fatal to his army."[54] On October 12, however, Grant approved the plan, observing that Sherman would, "no doubt, clean the country where you go of railroad tracks and supplies." Grant also advised him to take "every wagon, horse, mule, and hoof of stock, as well as the negroes."[55]

In selling the plan to his superiors, Sherman had implied that he would take Macon, the site of a Confederate arsenal, or Augusta, site of a gunpowder works. He and Grant also suggested that General Hood's army would probably follow Sherman, making a classic case for devastating a countryside to discourage pursuit.[56] In fact, Hood turned north to invade Tennessee, and Sherman avoided Macon and Augusta.

Sherman explained a more fundamental purpose for his march to his subordinate, General George Thomas: "I propose to demonstrate the vulnerability of the South, and make its inhabitants feel that war and individual ruin are synonymous terms."[57] During the march across Georgia, Sherman ordered that the "army will forage liberally on the country." Brigade commanders were to organize official foraging parties to gather "corn or forage of any kind, meat of any kind, vegetables, corn-meal, or whatever is needed by the command, aiming at all times to keep in the wagons at least ten days' provisions for the command and three days' forage." Soldiers were forbidden to "enter the dwellings of the inhabitants, or commit any trespass," but were "permitted to gather turnips, potatoes, and other vegetables, and to drive in stock in sight of their camp." Foragers were enjoined to "refrain from abusive or threatening language," and to "endeavor to leave with each family a reasonable portion for their maintenance."[58]

It has been pointed out that there was really little need to forage "liberally," since Sherman's army moved with a supply train of more than 2,500 wagons carrying a twenty-day supply of bread, and a cattle herd of 5,500 head that could provide beef rations for forty days.[59] If nothing else, however, liberal foraging impressed on Georgians "that war and individual ruin are synonymous terms." This was underscored when it became apparent to the soldiers that little effort would be made to enforce the rules against trespassing and refraining from threats. For example, after Union soldiers saw conditions at Camp Lawton, an abandoned Confederate prisoner of war camp, they burned the nearby town of Millen, whose inhabitants had nothing to do with the administration of the camp.[60] Nothing was done to punish the perpetrators, and some believed Sherman had personally authorized the town's destruction.

Union lack of discipline had become a way to make a political point about the powerlessness of the Confederate government. Sherman's orders also expressly permitted "devastation" in certain circumstances: "To army corps commanders alone is intrusted the power to destroy mills, houses, cotton-gins, &c., and for them this general principle is laid down: In districts and neighborhoods where the army is unmolested no destruction of such property should be permitted; but should guerrillas or bushwhackers molest our march, or should the inhabitants burn bridges, obstruct roads, or otherwise manifest local hostility, then army commanders should order and enforce a devastation more or less relentless according to the measure of such hostility."[61]

The one occasion when Sherman himself applied this order, in Sandersville, Georgia, went beyond traditional military practice. Sherman himself recounted the incident in his memoirs:

> A brigade of rebel cavalry was deployed before the town, and was driven in and through it by our skirmishers. I myself saw the rebel cavalry apply fire to stacks of fodder standing in the fields at Sandersville, and gave orders to burn some unoccupied

dwellings close by. On entering the town I told certain citizens (who would be sure to spread the report) that, if the enemy attempted to carry out their threat to burn their food, corn, and fodder, in our route, I would most undoubtedly execute to the letter the general orders of devastation made at the outset of the campaign.[62]

The Confederate destruction of forage at Sandersville was not the act of local civilians, guerrillas, or bushwhackers. It was a legitimate act of war carried out by regular Confederate cavalry, similar to acts that Grant and Sherman themselves had often authorized. Destroying houses was not, therefore, proper retaliation against the acts of unlawful belligerents, and it went beyond military necessity as that concept was and is usually understood. If it reflected any legal principle at all, it was a return to the primitive rule that all enemy property, public and private, could be taken or destroyed when captured. Deliberate nonenforcement of orders protecting private property reflected the same backward movement.

Were Sherman's plans known to President Lincoln and approved by him? As noted earlier, Sherman was not always completely candid with his superiors concerning his planned march to the sea. On one occasion, however, Sherman communicated his plans directly to the president. Ten days after the capture of Atlanta, while Sherman may have been at the height of optimism, he sent a telegram to the president excitedly describing favorable peace feelers from the Georgia political establishment. Governor Joseph Brown of Georgia had been at loggerheads with Confederate president Jefferson Davis for years, and had recently withdrawn the Georgia militia from Confederate military control. After the fall of Atlanta, the possibility had even been raised of Georgia rejoining the Union, or at least withdrawing all support for the government in Richmond:

A Mr Wright, former member of Congress from Rome Ga and a Mr King of Marietta are now going between Gov Brown and myself—I have said that some of the people of Georgia are now engaged in rebellion began in error and perpetrated in pride; but that Georgia can now save herself from the devastation of War preparing for her only by withdrawing her quota out of the Confederate Army, and aiding me to repel Hood from the border of the State; in which event *instead of desolating the land,*

as we progress I will keep our men to the high roads and commons,
and pay for the corn and meat we need and take. I am fully con-
scious of the delicate nature of such assertions, but it would be
a magnificent stroke of policy, if I could without wasting a foot
of ground or of principle arouse the latent enmity to Jeff Davis,
of Georgia.[63]

Politically this all came to nothing, and Georgia suffered Sherman's
march to the sea. What is interesting is Sherman's description of his
military options in case of a compromise—"instead of desolating the
land, as we progress I will keep our men to the high roads and commons, and pay for the corn and meat we need and take." "Desolating the
land" was described as the necessary result of Sherman not keeping his
troops together on the "high roads." How would Lincoln have understood the "desolation" implied by allowing soldiers to roam and forage
freely over the Georgia countryside? This was one of the few instances
that, as president, Abraham Lincoln could draw on his limited military
experience thirty years earlier in the Black Hawk War.

Black Hawk was the leader of a faction of the Fox and Sauk Indian nations who rejected an 1816 treaty ceding to the United States
their traditional homeland along the Rock River of Illinois. In April
1832, he led about a thousand followers, half of whom were warriors,
from Iowa back across the Mississippi in an attempt to reoccupy these
lands.[64] Governor John Reynolds of Illinois called out the state militia, and among the volunteers from Sangamon County was the young
Abraham Lincoln.

Though he never saw combat, Lincoln served in three different militia units. From April 21 to May 27, he served as a captain in command
of a company of infantry. He then re-enlisted for twenty days as a private in a cavalry company commanded by Elijah Iles. He re-enlisted for
a third time in another cavalry company led by Jacob Early, a Springfield physician and minister.[65]

The war ended in predictable disaster for Black Hawk's followers,
but it raised Abraham Lincoln's social status in frontier Illinois. He had
been elected a militia captain with the support of a local group of ruffians known as the "Clary's Grove boys," but this nevertheless made
him an "officer and a gentleman" in military law and social tradition.
Although he served as a private in Iles's and Early's companies, the cavalry was regarded as a having a higher social status than the infantry.[66]

Lincoln has traditionally been portrayed as a reluctant soldier, but it has been pointed out that only 5 percent of the Sangamon Country militiamen re-enlisted for three tours of duty as he did. It is hard to picture Abraham Lincoln as a "spit and polish" peacetime soldier; nevertheless, something appealed to him about service in the field. Recalling these experiences as president may have helped him form the deep bond of sympathy that he had with the enlisted men of the Union army.

However Lincoln's personal status may have risen, the Illinois militiamen he encountered in 1832 were far more undisciplined than Sherman's veterans of 1864. William Cullen Bryant, visiting his brother in Illinois at the time, described the 1832 militia as "a hard-looking set of men, unkempt and unshaven."[67] Bryant's opinion may be disregarded as that of an effete Eastern poet, but Lincoln's Illinois contemporaries also described the men in his New Salem company as "a hard set of men all fighting stock" and "the hardest set of men I ever saw."[68] A regular army officer found the Illinois militia to be marked by "weakness, waste and confusion." The militiamen took rail fences from local farms for firewood and stole pigs, chickens, and garden vegetables (acts that would have been familiar to any farmer in the vicinity of a Civil War army). They allowed their horses to graze on planted fields. One farmer complained to military authorities that the militia had ruined ten acres of oats, four acres of corn, one half acre of wheat, and three-fourths of an acre of potatoes. Another, who lived near the site of the former chief village of the Fox Indians, claimed that he had lost twenty acres of corn and potatoes. The soldiers, he concluded, had caused him "ten times as much damage as the Indians had ever done."[69]

Lincoln personally encountered at least one such episode. In 1867, one of his former comrades in arms wrote to William Herndon that the militiamen once came across a new cabin whose owners had "vacated and [skedaddled] for fear they would lose their scalps, and there were plenty of chickens about said cabin . . . and the boys heard a voice saying 'slay and eat' so they went to shooting, clubbing & running them as long as any could be found." The narrator himself explored the farm's smokehouse and found the "cleanest sweetest" jowl of bacon he had ever seen. Lincoln came across the group when they were finishing the food and remarked, "Eating chicken boys?" "Not much sir," was the reply. Lincoln was then offered what remained of the bacon. "He ate bacon fat . . . saying to them many funny remarks." That the narrator remembered twice addressing Lincoln as "sir" suggests the incident occurred while he was still captain of the company.[70]

Thirty years later, when General Sherman wrote to the president that his soldiers would "desolate" Georgia if not kept to the high roads, the images that came to Lincoln's mind would have been based on these experiences. He would have expected Sherman's men to wage a war on pigs, chickens, and vegetables, to trample crops, take fence rails, and commit similar acts of minor hooliganism, just as his militiamen had. Armies on both sides of the Civil War were doing that type of damage daily, and he would have seen no reason to interfere with the march on that basis. Lincoln would not have anticipated the burnings at Millen and Sandersville. These would have appeared to the president as mere acts of revenge, which he had always opposed.

Lincoln's experiences as a militia officer may also explain his reaction to the case of Colonel John Basil Turchin. The son of a Cossack officer, Turchin was born in Russia in 1822. Following family tradition, he attended the Nicholas Academy of the General Staff, Russia's most prestigious military school, and thereafter served on the Staff of the Imperial Guards. Turchin and his wife emigrated to the United States in 1856, and at the outbreak of the Civil War he was working for the Illinois Central Railroad in Chicago. As an experienced European officer, he was quickly given command of the Nineteenth Illinois Infantry, and he later commanded a brigade in General Don Carlos Buell's Army of the Ohio.[71]

In the spring of 1862, Turchin's brigade was stationed in northern Alabama. Bridge burning, bushwhacking, and other harassment from guerrillas had increased tensions between the soldiers and the local population. On the night of May 1, Confederate cavalrymen attacked one of Turchin's regiments stationed in Athens, Alabama, and local civilians joined in driving the Union troops out of town. Turchin's brigade retook Athens the following day. His troops, some of whom believed that Turchin wanted the town sacked, looted several stores on the town square, and a slave girl was allegedly raped in front of her mistress. The looting began while Colonel Turchin was still at the square, though he later denied any knowledge of it.[72]

General Buell ordered Turchin court-martialed for dereliction of duty and conduct unbecoming an officer. At the trial, Turchin and his counsel argued that no evidence was presented that he had authorized or known of the looting, and that he could not monitor the behavior of his troops because other pressing duties required his attention outside the town. After the rape was reported to him, he had arrested the suspected soldier and sent him to Buell's headquarters at Huntsville.[73]

As was customary, the accused was given the opportunity to make a final unsworn statement to the seven members of the court-martial. Turchin spoke for an hour and a half, denying the charges against him. He concluded by attacking the conciliatory policies of General Buell. "The more lenient we are with secessionists," the *New York Times* reported him as saying, "the more insolent they become; and if we do not prosecute this war using all the means we can bring to bear against the enemy, including the emancipation of slaves, the ruin of this country is inevitable."[74]

Colonel Turchin was found guilty and sentenced to be dismissed from the service. Six of the seven members of the court-martial signed a clemency petition, but General Buell, no doubt doubly irritated that Turchin had used the trial as a platform to attack Buell's policies, nevertheless approved the findings and sentence. Turchin's wife traveled to Washington to appeal for clemency, amid growing popular support for Turchin in the North, starting in his home town of Chicago. Though irrelevant as a matter of law, Turchin's attack on lenient treatment of enemy property struck a chord with the public, and there were widespread calls for the president to pardon or reinstate him.

Clemency came, but in an unexpected form. On August 2, 1862, the War Department announced that Turchin had been promoted to brigadier general, with a date of rank from the middle of July, before his trial. Since a court-martial had to be composed of officers higher in rank than the accused, the promotion had the legal effect of voiding the court-martial findings and sentence. Instead of pleading for her husband's reinstatement, Nadine Turchin found herself accepting his commission as a general officer and taking it back to Chicago.[75] When Illinois governor Richard Yates wrote to ask that Turchin be restored to active duty and again placed in command of a brigade, President Lincoln approved the request.[76]

It has been argued that Lincoln's approval of Turchin's return to command marked a change in policy toward the property of Southern civilians.[77] This probably reads too much into it. The change in policy, allowing Federal armies to live off the land, had been published by the War Department on July 22. At his cabinet meeting on the same date, the president had already announced his decision to issue an emancipation proclamation, as Turchin called for in his unsworn statement, and was awaiting only a Union military victory to issue it.

That Lincoln and Turchin agreed on adopting strong "hard war" measures does not, however, explain why the president would ignore the findings of Turchin's court-martial. The looting of Athens was clearly an act of revenge, which the president consistently opposed. The president was also consistently unsympathetic to Union soldiers convicted of rape.

The most straightforward explanation is that the president agreed with Turchin's defense that he should not be punished for what his men did without his permission. From Lincoln's short service as a militia officer thirty years earlier, he would have recalled how difficult it was to control Western volunteer soldiers and bring them under military discipline. General Buell was being particularly disingenuous in charging Turchin with dereliction of duty in handling the rape case. Colonel Turchin had the suspect arrested and sent up the chain of command for court-martial proceedings, but someone at Buell's headquarters decided to drop the charges. A successful prosecution would have required the slave victim to testify against a white soldier. This was probably considered too inflammatory to the white people of Alabama, even if the accused was a Yankee.[78] The suspected rapist was returned to his regiment.

When we consider Colonel Turchin's responsibility for his soldiers' acts and President Lincoln's responsibility for the acts of Sherman, Turchin, and other officers, the risk of "presentism" is especially great. Since World War II, the law of war has developed a widely known principle of "command responsibility," which holds that under certain circumstances a commanding officer can be held legally liable for crimes committed by his subordinates, even when the commander did not authorize the acts.[79] This concept was unknown when the Civil War was fought. The first hint that superior officers had an affirmative duty to prevent crimes by their soldiers does not appear until 1899, when the Hague Convention on Land Warfare required the parties to the convention to "issue instructions to their armed land forces" to ensure that the terms of the convention were carried out.[80] The current version of the principle was codified as follows in a Protocol Additional to the Geneva Conventions: "The fact that a breach of the Conventions or of this Protocol was committed by a subordinate does not absolve his superiors from penal . . . responsibility, . . . if they knew, or had information which should have enabled them to conclude in the circumstances at the time, that he was committing or was going to commit such a breach and if they did not take all feasible measures within their power to prevent or repress the breach."[81] Even under this modern standard, it can be argued that Colonel Turchin should not be liable for the acts of his soldiers at Athens, Alabama. He did take feasible precautions to prevent or repress disorder by appointing an officer as provost marshal, with the duty of keeping order in the town, and took action to prosecute the suspected rapists once the crimes were reported to him. In the case of President Lincoln and General Sherman in Georgia, based on the general's very limited sharing of plans with Washington, Lincoln had no reason to expect more damage to civilian property than would be normal whenever a Civil War army moved through a populated countryside.

5

"Can You Get Near Enough to Throw Shells into the City?"

Personal Injury to Civilians

When President Lincoln wrote the order of April 25, 1861, authorizing bombardment of Baltimore, he may not have realized the full implications of the power he was giving General Winfield Scott. Errors in the order that are apparent when the full text is read suggest that it was written in haste and excitement:

> The Maryland Legislature assembles to-morrow at Anapolis; and, not improbably, will take action to arm the people of that State against the United States. The question has been submitted to, and considered by me, whether it would not be justifiable, upon the ground of necessary defence, for you, as commander in Chief of the United States Army, to arrest, or disperse the members of that body. I think it would *not* be justifiable; nor, efficient for the desired object.
>
> First, they have a clearly legal right to assemble; and, we can not know in advance, that their action will not be lawful, and peaceful. And if we wait until they shall *have* acted, their arrest, or dispersion, will not lessen the effect of their action.
>
> Secondly, we *can* not permanently prevent their action. If we arrest them, we can not long hold them as prisoners; and when liberated, they will immediately re-assemble, and take their action. And, precisely the same if we simply disperse them. They will immediately re-assemble in some other place.
>
> I therefore conclude that it is only left to the Commanding

General to watch, and await their action, which, if it shall be to arm their people against the United States, he is to adopt the most prompt, and efficient means to counteract, even, if necessary, to the bombardment of their cities—and in the extreme necessity, the suspension of the writ of habeas corpus.[1]

"Annapolis" is misspelled in the first paragraph, and the last paragraph, read literally, implies that suspension of habeas corpus was a more serious act than bombardment. Also in the last paragraph, Lincoln initially wrote "*suspicion* of the writ of habeas corpus" rather than "suspension of the writ of habeas corpus." The president's secretaries, John Nicolay and John Hay, later remembered that during this period Lincoln, "by nature and habit so calm," was "in a state of nervous tension which put all his great powers of mental and physical endurance to their severest trial."[2]

General Scott probably requested authorization to bombard disloyal cities in Maryland. He had experience dealing with hostile cities during the war with Mexico. The final, and successful, campaign of that war began on March 9, 1847, when his troops landed on the Gulf coast of Mexico near Vera Cruz. Scott's plan was to march rapidly inland and capture Mexico City, forcing the Mexican government to sue for peace, but first he had to capture the fortified city of Vera Cruz. After a formal call for surrender had been refused, Scott began bombarding the city on March 22, using heavy naval cannon, mortars, and rockets. During the next four days, 6,700 rounds of shot and shell, weighing 463,000 pounds, fell on the city and its fortifications. On March 25, the consuls of France, England, and Prussia proposed a truce to allow evacuation of women and children. Scott refused. The request was repeated on the 26th and again refused. (In his memoirs, Scott explained that he could not afford any delay in taking the city because tropical fever was already breaking out in his army and there were reports that a Mexican relief force was being organized.)[3] Negotiations for surrender followed, and the city capitulated on March 27.

The aiming point for the American bombardment was the powder magazine of the chief Mexican fort, but inevitably, given the inaccuracy of mid-nineteenth-century artillery, most of the ordnance fell on the city, populated by 15,000 civilians. Although the black powder artillery shells of the Mexican and Civil wars were not nearly as effective as munitions developed in the twentieth century, there were civilian casualties. A British naval officer on the scene estimated that 80 Mexican soldiers and 100 civilians had been killed at Vera Cruz.[4]

Scott's actions were not as callous as might initially appear. He could not advance on the Mexican capital with his relatively small force of 12,000 men and leave a heavily fortified enemy city in his rear. As one of his biographers has pointed out, he had three options: he could try to take the city by direct assault, try to bombard it into submission, or try to starve out the garrison. The first option would not only cause heavy casualties for his own small force, but also expose the civilian population to the risks of urban combat and the real possibility of pillage, rape, and murder if Scott's officers lost control of their men; the volunteer militia units that made up most of his army were poorly disciplined to begin with. Starvation would give the Mexican government time to organize a relief column, and would probably have the worst impact on civilians of any of the choices (in a siege, armed soldiers are always the last to go hungry). Scott had good reason to conclude that bombardment was the best course of action from both a military and a humanitarian standpoint.

It was with this background that General Scott received President Lincoln's order on April 25, 1861. If Maryland seceded, he might again be faced with the same choices he had to make before Vera Cruz, only this time he would have to reduce an American city to obedience. If that time came, the president had at least approved one of his possible options—bombardment.

In the end, of course, Maryland did not secede and Baltimore was not bombarded. Union troops found an alternative route to Washington and the New York Seventh Regiment entered the capital on the day Lincoln gave Scott his orders. Still, the threat of bombardment played a role in resolving the crisis. Baltimore was not finally subdued until May 13, when Massachusetts general Benjamin Butler occupied Federal Hill, overlooking Baltimore harbor, and trained cannon on the city.

It was not until more than a year later that President Lincoln again considered the bombardment of a hostile city. In the intervening period he had developed more confidence in his own military judgment. In April 1861, he had passively authorized General Scott to make the decision. In May 1862, he actively encouraged General George McClellan to bombard the Confederate capital at Richmond.

McClellan was appointed to command Federal forces around Washington, D.C., in August 1861, following the debacle at the First Battle of Bull Run. He reorganized and reinvigorated the beaten troops and renamed them the Army of the Potomac. He also earned a reputation as a skilled administrator but an overly cautious combat commander. Lincoln's frustration with McClellan's reluctance to attack the Confederates steadily grew in the fall of 1861. In March 1862, McClellan finally started to move the Army of the Potomac to the Virginia Peninsula, between the York and James rivers, preparatory to an advance on Richmond. Lincoln's frustration returned when McClellan's advance up the peninsula proceeded at his usual methodical rate.

In letters to his wife, General McClellan referred to the president as "a well meaning baboon," "the Gorilla," and an "idiot."[5] Holding these views, he naturally considered Lincoln's frequent visits to his headquarters as an irritation rather than an opportunity to win the president's support. He probably assumed that he would be free of Lincoln's constant prodding once he and his army were safely on the peninsula and far from Washington. (He had earlier moved his headquarters from Washington, D.C., to Alexandria, Virginia, but the Potomac River proved an insufficient barrier to continued presidential visits.)

Unfortunately for McClellan, a telegraph line connected Washington with Fortress Monroe at the tip of the peninsula, and the Army Signal Corps kept Fortress Monroe connected to the slowly moving headquarters of the Army of the Potomac. The president made generous use of the new technology to keep track of the general's plans and the progress of the army.[6] On May 26, McClellan's headquarters received the following telegraphic inquiry:

> Can you not cut the Aquia Creek Railroad? Also, what impression have you as to intrenched works for you to contend with in front of Richmond? Can you get near enough to throw shells into the city?
>
> A. Lincoln, President[7]

In the Shenandoah Valley, a hundred miles northwest of the Confederate capital, Stonewall Jackson had just won two battles against Union general Nathaniel Banks. These Confederate victories increased the possibility of an attack on President Lincoln's own capital, and he probably wondered how much longer it would take the Army of the Potomac to reduce Richmond. McClellan replied the same day as follows:

Have cut the Virginia Central Rail Road in three places, between Hanover C[ourt] H[ouse] and the Chickahominy
[River]. Will try to cut the other. I do not think Richmond
entrenchments formidable, but am not certain. Hope very soon
to be within shelling distance. . . .

G. B. McClellan.[8]

Several interesting aspects of this brief interchange should be noted. First, the president did not ask when McClellan could use his heavy
guns against the defenses or entrenchments of Richmond; he was interested in throwing shells "into the city." Second, though McClellan was
one of the prime proponents of a "soft war" toward Southern civilians,
he raised no objection to this suggestion and implied that he was ready
to carry it out. Shortly after taking command in August 1861, McClellan advised the president that he intended to pursue "a rigidly protective
policy as to private property and unarmed persons."[9] On July 7, 1862,
he would submit another memorandum to Lincoln, urging that the war
be "conducted upon the highest principles known to Christian Civilization," and should not be transformed into "a War upon population."[10]
For McClellan, the highest principles of Christian civilization forbade
the emancipation of slaves. They did not, apparently, forbid throwing
heavy artillery and mortar shells into a city of more than 40,000 people.

General McClellan never got the chance to find out how effective his siege guns would have been against Richmond. Five days after
the telegraph exchange with President Lincoln, when McClellan was
only twelve miles from the city, his army was attacked by General Joe
Johnston at the battle of Seven Pines (also known as Fair Oaks). After
Johnston was wounded, Robert E. Lee took command of the army defending Richmond, and during the Seven Days' Battles (June 25–July
1, 1862) drove McClellan back to Harrison's Landing on the James
River.

It fell to a Confederate general to first bombard a defended town
in the Civil War. On September 4, 1862, Robert E. Lee began his first
invasion of the North, moving the Army of Northern Virginia across
the Potomac River toward Frederick, Maryland. At Frederick, Lee
learned that the Federal garrison at Harper's Ferry, near his line of communication up the Shenandoah Valley, had not abandoned its position
as expected. Unwilling to leave a hostile force in his rear, he sent half
his army, under General Stonewall Jackson, to capture Harper's Ferry.

Lee's plans called for Harper's Ferry to be quickly reduced before the Federal Army of the Potomac could attack the separated parts of his army piecemeal. Three hills—Bolivar Heights, Loudon Heights, and Maryland Heights—overlooked Harper's Ferry, and by the morning of September 14, Jackson had Confederate artillery on Loudon and Maryland Heights and his main force faced the Federal defenders occupying Bolivar Heights. Any cannon on Maryland Heights would be in a good position to bombard the town itself, and at 7:20 A.M. on September 14, Jackson sent the following orders to General Lafayette McLaws, commanding the Confederate force there: "So soon as you get your batteries all planted, let me know, as I desire, after yourself, Walker [on Loudon Heights], and myself have our batteries ready to open, to send in a flag of truce, for the purpose of getting out the non-combatants, should the commanding officer refuse to surrender. Should we have to attack, let the work be done thoroughly; fire on the houses when necessary. The citizens can keep out of harm's way from your artillery. Demolish the place if it is occupied by the enemy, and does not surrender."[11] By September 1862 there were probably few, if any, civilian "citizens" left in Harper's Ferry, but Jackson had no way of knowing that. He would know that any civilians who were endangered by McLaws's guns would likely be pro-Confederate Virginians rather than Yankees. Moreover, since Jackson had earlier commanded a Confederate garrison at Harper's Ferry, he might well personally have known some of the civilians he was placing in harm's way.

Fortunately for the Confederate cause, Jackson did not have the opportunity to offer the enemy a twenty-four-hour truce. (With an extra twenty-four hours, the Sixth Corps of the Army of the Potomac might well have captured McLaws and lifted the siege of Harper's Ferry.) Before Jackson could send a flag of truce, Union artillery began firing at General John Walker's battery on Loudon Heights. Walker returned fire and was soon joined by McLaws's guns. Once the battle had started, Jackson abandoned his intent to allow civilians to leave the besieged area, but his orders to "fire on the houses when necessary" and to "demolish the place" still stood. The Union garrison surrendered after a day and night of intense bombardment.

Nothing better illustrates how the laws and customs of war have changed between the nineteenth and twenty-first centuries than the bombardment of civilians in besieged towns. Today, it is accepted that attacks on a civilian population, as such, are prohibited, and that even attacks on legitimate military objectives should be canceled if the expected civilian casualties would be excessive or disproportionate to the expected military advantage.[12]

In the nineteenth century, however, no similar rules applied to civilians in a town under siege. When a town or city was fortified, the entire town, including civilian residential areas, was a legitimate military objective.[13] One theory behind this rule was that if the civilian inhabitants and their property were placed in danger, they would put pressure on the defending commander to surrender or negotiate for terms.

Jackson, McClellan, and Scott were all professional soldiers, well aware of the customary standards of their time. Winfield Scott was a law student before he entered the army and had widely studied and even translated European military treatises. McClellan was a military engineer who had served under General Scott at the siege of Vera Cruz and considered Scott the general under whom he had "learned the art of war."[14] As an official observer for the U.S. Army, he witnessed the siege of Sevastopol by French and British armies during the Crimean War. Jackson had been professor of artillery at the Virginia Military Institute, and President Lincoln had spent the fall and winter of 1861–1862 studying military literature from the Library of Congress.

Contemporary legal authorities agreed with the military. The favorite authority on international law among American lawyers and judges of the early nineteenth century was the eighteenth-century Swiss writer Emmerich de Vattel, whose *Law of Nations* was cited more than any other work.[15] Vattel summarized the rules of bombardment as follows: "To destroy a town with bombs and red-hot balls, is an extremity to which we do not proceed without cogent reasons. But it is nevertheless warranted by the laws of war, when we are unable by any other mode to reduce an important post, on which the success of the war may depend, or which enables the enemy to annoy us in a dangerous manner."[16] There was an echo of Vattel's reference to red-hot cannonballs in later Civil War sieges, when incendiary shells were used against Vicksburg and Charleston, though without much practical effect. President Lincoln took a personal interest in the development of these munitions, and one historian has suggested this interest evidenced a humanitarian deficiency in Lincoln's nature.[17] Indeed, during the siege of Charleston President Lincoln once asked a visiting delegation of army officers why they were not shelling the city; they replied that they preferred to save ammunition to support another attack on the city's fortified defenses.[18]

It should be noted, however, that as late as 1956, the U.S. Army's manual on the law of war asserted that it was not illegal to use incendiary munitions, even against targets in cities.[19] The most recent treaty on the use of incendiaries, concluded in 1980, prohibits only the use of air-dropped incendiary bombs against targets in cities and other concentrations of civilians. Incendiary artillery shells, like those used in Civil War sieges, are still lawful if directed against military targets and if other precautions are taken.[20]

Similarly, Stonewall Jackson was under no legal obligation to allow civilians to leave Harper's Ferry before his attack, and Winfield Scott was clearly within his rights to refuse an exit to noncombatants at Vera Cruz. In April 1863, the U.S. government issued the Lieber Code, a summary of the laws and customs of war, as then understood, for the guidance of Union forces. The Lieber Code stated that it was "lawful to starve the hostile belligerent, armed or unarmed, so that it leads to the speedier subjection of the enemy," and that "when a commander of a besieged place expels the noncombatants, in order to lessen the number of those who consume his stock of provisions, it is lawful, though an extreme measure, to drive them back, so as to hasten on the surrender."[21]

This rule had a remarkable longevity, and was still cited and applied well into the twentieth century. The U.S. Army's official guidance on the laws and customs of war in World War I affirmed that there was "no rule of law which compels the commander of an investing force to authorize the population, including women, children, aged, sick, wounded, subjects of neutral powers, or temporary residents to leave the besieged locality," citing as precedents Scott's conduct at Vera Cruz and Japanese practice during the Russo-Japanese War. It then repeated Lieber's statement that it was lawful to drive back noncombatants forced to leave a besieged place.[22]

During the siege of Leningrad in World War II, German field marshal Wilhelm von Leeb approved orders directing his artillery to fire at civilians trying to flee the city. After the war, he was accused of various war crimes, including the approval of this order, and brought before a U.S. military tribunal. Based on the rule codified by Lieber, he was found not guilty of this charge. The tribunal observed, "We might wish the law were otherwise but we must administer it as we find it."[23]

Following World War II, the 1949 Geneva Convention on Civilians tried to mitigate the rule that Scott followed at Vera Cruz by providing that "parties to the conflict shall endeavour to conclude local agreements for the removal from besieged or encircled areas, of wounded, sick, infirm, and aged persons, children and maternity cases, and for the passage of ministers of all religions, medical personnel and medical equipment on their way to such areas."[24] Nevertheless, the 1956 U.S. Army manual on the law of war stated that if no "local agreement" to the contrary had been reached, it was still in the discretion of the besieging commander whether to allow noncombatants to leave a besieged locality, and that it was still "lawful, though an extreme measure," to force expelled noncombatants to return.[25]

These were the rules applied in later sieges of the Civil War—Atlanta, Charleston, Petersburg, and Vicksburg. "I was not bound by the laws of war to give notice of the shelling of Atlanta," snapped William T. Sherman to Confederate general John Bell Hood. "See the books."[26] Sherman was right. The law books of the 1860s were on his side, as they would have been on the side of Scott at Vera Cruz and Stonewall Jackson at Harper's Ferry.

Although the black-powder shells used in Civil War sieges were much less destructive than later munitions, indiscriminate bombardment of civilian areas may have been a moral "blind spot" of the Victorian era, common to Europeans and to Americans on both sides of the Civil War.[27] The blind spot nevertheless existed and must be taken into account when judging the actions of Civil War military commanders, North and South, including those of Commander in Chief Abraham Lincoln.

There is a continuing debate over whether the Civil War was the first "modern war" or "total war," the precursor of the world wars of the twentieth century.[28] Most historians agree, however, that in one crucial respect the Civil War differed from the total wars of the last century. Except in retaliation for unlawful acts of the enemy, the organized armies on both sides did not target civilians for deliberate killing.[29] Inhabitants of the Warsaw Ghetto, Nanking, or Tokyo in World War II, or Rwanda and the former Yugoslavia in the 1990s, surely would gladly have exchanged places with Southern civilians in the path of Hunter, Sherman, or Sheridan in 1864.

Nevertheless, Lincoln was acquainted with one form of total war in the twentieth-century sense. Mark Neely has suggested that whereas the Civil War was generally waged within the existing laws of war, Indian wars in the United States often took on the characteristics of total war. Of this Lincoln had some knowledge from personal experience and family tradition.[30]

As he recalled in the short autobiography he wrote for Jesse Fell, his grandfather Abraham Lincoln had been killed in Kentucky by Indians in the 1780s, "not in battle, but by stealth, when he was laboring to open a farm in the forest."[31] He saw the other side of the Indian wars while serving as a militia captain in the Black Hawk War. At one point, Lincoln and his men passed through an abandoned Indian village and saw a display of scalps of white women and children, including one scalp of an old woman, as well as the fetus cut from the body of a dead woman. "Strong men wept at this," one militiaman recalled years later, "hard hearted men cried."[32] The militia were primed for revenge when an elderly Indian man entered their camp with an old document attesting to his good character signed by Lewis Cass, governor of the Michigan Territory before 1831. Most of the men wanted to shoot him, either as a spy or just because he was an Indian, but Lincoln prevented them, placing himself between the old man and the militiamen.[33] From early in his life, then, killing for revenge was not Lincoln's way, even in a primitive "total war" between settlers and Indians.

As president, Lincoln again had occasion to interfere with killing Indians for revenge. Perhaps Lincoln's most unpopular humanitarian act was his response to the aftermath of the 1862 Sioux Indian uprising in Minnesota.[34] Many Sioux in that state were close to starvation in the summer of 1862 due to crop failures and bureaucratic delay in providing supplies guaranteed by treaty. Hostilities opened on August 17, when four young men demanded food from a white farm family and the confrontation ended with the killing of five settlers. Fearing white reprisals for this incident, the Minnesota Sioux went to war.

Exaggerated report of massacres appeared in the press, and the state governor demanded military action from Washington, claiming that half the population had become refugees. On September 5, Major General John Pope was ordered to take command against the Sioux. On October 9, he reported that the Sioux war was at an end, with the army holding about 1,500 Indian prisoners. General Pope ordered that military commissions try any who were suspected of participating in the uprising, and within a month more than 300 had been sentenced to death. Pope intended to carry out the sentences with dispatch, but persons sympathetic to the Indians protested against the mass execution. Lincoln's own commissioner of Indian affairs wrote to the secretary of the interior that the "indiscriminate punishment of men who have laid down their arms and surrendered themselves as prisoners, partakes more of the character of revenge than the infliction of deserved punishment."[35] On November 10, President Lincoln ordered that no executions be carried out until he could review the records of trial.

In most cases, these records were shockingly inadequate. Most of the military commission proceedings were not real trials but merely added a color of legality to executions for revenge. Although the death sentences were highly popular among Minnesota voters, Lincoln nevertheless approved executions in only thirty-nine cases. In those cases the evidence indicated either rape or the killing of noncombatants.[36]

The Minnesota Sioux were not the only objects of vengeance in the Civil War. Revenge killings were endemic to the guerrilla conflicts in Kentucky and Missouri. In the latter state, affairs reached a nadir in the spring of 1864 as Confederate irregulars and pro-Union vigilantes waged a war of mutual atrocity. Southern sympathizers were routinely "roused from sleep at night, dragged from their homes by Unionist death squads and murdered before the eyes of their horrified families."[37]

As rumors of revenge killings by Unionist vigilantes trickled into Washington, President Lincoln knew that the Missouri situation would have to be handled by a talented but deeply flawed commander on the scene, Major General William Rosecrans, who had the misfortune to command the Military Department of the Missouri in 1864. The army in Missouri was highly politicized. Rosecrans had reported to Lincoln that although his two principal subordinates were both "good fighting men," they were so "mixed up in local politics that all their actions will be suspected if not charged, by the opposite side to proceed from party bias."[38] In this paranoid atmosphere, suspicions naturally arose that the Union high command approved of the Unionist death squads.

In typical fashion, Lincoln chose to be diplomatic and tactful with a general facing a very difficult mission, and to whom he did, after all, owe a debt of gratitude for the 1863 victory at Murfreesboro. In April Lincoln wrote a letter to Rosecrans that he described as "rather more social than official, containing suggestions rather than orders." Raising the delicate issue of revenge killings, he made it clear that these would not be tolerated: "It is said, I know not whether truly, that in some parts of Missouri, assassinations are systematically committed upon returned rebels, who wish to ground arms, and behave themselves. This should not be. Of course I have not heard that you give countenance to, or wink at such assassinations."[39] To reassure Rosecrans of the president's continued confidence, Lincoln closed with a compliment that was, in retrospect, rather backhanded: "So far you have got along in the Department of the Missouri, rather better than I dared to hope; and I congratulate you and myself upon it."

In war there may be other reasons to kill civilians aside from revenge. As the Civil War went into its fourth year, David Herbert Donald has noted, "a grim streak of ruthless determination, not hitherto noticeable, began to appear in Lincoln's character."[40] It has been argued that this ruthless streak went so far that Lincoln authorized the assassination of Confederate president Jefferson Davis and his entire cabinet.

The assassination, it is alleged, was to be carried out in early 1864 during a cavalry raid on Richmond, Virginia, led by General Judson Kilpatrick and Colonel Ulric Dahlgren.[41] The overt purpose of the raid was to free Union prisoners of war being held on Belle Isle in Richmond. Late in the summer of 1863, in response to the Confederate refusal to treat captured African American soldiers as prisoners of war, President Lincoln ordered an end to prisoner exchanges.[42] Political pressure on the president grew throughout the fall, as friends and relatives of captured Union soldiers demanded that the government reinstate exchanges, or at any rate do something effective to free white prisoners of war.

General Kilpatrick, commanding a cavalry division in the Army of the Potomac, believed he had an answer to the president's prisoner dilemma. Believing Richmond to be lightly defended, he proposed to lead a large cavalry force around the flank of Lee's army to attack the city from the northeast. While Kilpatrick's force distracted the defenders, a smaller force would enter Richmond from the west, capture the prison camp at Belle Isle, and join forces with Kilpatrick. The reunited force would then escort the freed prisoners, perhaps as many as 10,000, to the Union lines at Williamsburg before J. E. B. Stuart's Confederate cavalry could respond. Secondary missions of the raiders would include cutting several railroads serving Richmond and destroying a nearby Confederate arsenal.[43] Incidentally, a successful raid would also cover Kilpatrick with personal glory. Working around his superiors in the Army of the Potomac (who did not like him and had a low opinion of his talents), Kilpatrick arranged an interview directly with President Lincoln.

The president enthusiastically approved the plan and added an additional mission for the raid. In December, he had issued an amnesty proclamation, aimed at ordinary citizens in the Confederate States.[44]

He hoped that as a weapon of psychological warfare, this would have an impact similar to that of the Emancipation Proclamation. Just as the latter had weakened the Confederacy by undermining economic support from slaves, the amnesty proclamation might draw free white men back to the Union.[45] Concerned that the proclamation was not reaching its intended audience, Lincoln proposed that the raiding party distribute copies along their route. With this additional mission, Lincoln passed Kilpatrick on to Secretary of War Stanton to work out the details of the raid.

At some point the raid came to the attention of Colonel Ulric Dahlgren. Dahlgren had high-level political connections and arranged to have himself appointed to command the smaller force that would enter Richmond from the west and liberate the prisoners. Dahlgren's father, John A. Dahlgren, was a close friend of the president's, having been commandant of the Washington navy yard during the first two years of his administration. Lincoln and the elder Dahlgren shared an interest in technology, and during this period the president often visited the navy yard to witness the testing of new weapons with the commandant.

At age twenty-two, Ulric Dahlgren had a personality considerably more daring than his father's. Attached to the headquarters of the Army of the Potomac, he enjoyed working behind Confederate lines, alone or with a few followers, and in today's military he would undoubtedly have volunteered for the Navy SEALS or a similar elite special operations force. On November 10, 1862, he slipped into Fredericksburg with a small band of scouts and captured part of the Confederate garrison.[46] During the 1863 Gettysburg campaign, Dahlgren scored a major intelligence coup by capturing a courier bearing a message from Jefferson Davis telling General Lee he would receive no reinforcements. During the Confederate retreat from Gettysburg, he led a rag-tag group of Pennsylvania cavalry and civilian volunteers on a raid against Lee's supply train that destroyed more than 160 wagons.[47] He was wounded trying to enter Hagerstown, Maryland, while it was occupied by Lee's forces, necessitating the amputation of his leg. Despite loss of a limb, he seemed the perfect officer to lead a desperate attack on the enemy capital with fewer than 500 men.

Under Kilpatrick's command, 4,000 of the best cavalrymen and mounts in the Army of the Potomac, supported by a battery of light artillery, moved out on February 28, 1864.[48] Dahlgren's party of 460 troopers split off as scheduled, but from that point on the fortunes of war went against the raiders. On March 1, Kilpatrick found the Richmond defenses manned by more formidable troops than the elderly militia and home guards he had expected, and turned back. Dahlgren's African American guide could not locate a practicable ford across the James River, an offense for which Dahlgren had him summarily hanged.

On March 2, as he attempted to return to the Army of the Potomac, Colonel Dahlgren's party was ambushed by the enemy and Dahlgren was killed. On his body the Confederate authorities found papers that they claimed revealed plans of "an extraordinary and diabolical character," far beyond liberating prisoners and burning an arsenal.[49] According to a draft address by Dahlgren to his men, they were to "cross the James River into Richmond, destroying the bridges after us and exhorting the released prisoners to destroy and burn the hateful city; and do not allow the rebel leader Davis and his traitorous crew to escape." More damning still, according to draft orders found on the body, "the men must keep together and well in hand, and once in the city it must be destroyed and Jeff. Davis and cabinet killed."[50]

A grieving Admiral Dahlgren denounced the papers as forgeries, and Union officers, speaking to the press, denied that any such orders had been given or suggested.[51] On April 15, Robert E. Lee, on instructions from his government, sent a note by flag of truce to General George Gordon Meade, commander of the Army of the Potomac, requesting an official U.S. response to the papers. "In obedience to my instructions," Lee wrote, "I beg leave respectfully to inquire whether the designs and instructions of Colonel Dahlgren, as set forth in these papers, . . . were authorized by the United States Government or by his superior officers, and also whether they have the sanction and approval of those authorities." Meade replied to General Lee two days later "that neither the United States Government, myself, nor General Kilpatrick authorized, sanctioned, or approved the burning of the city of Richmond and the killing of Mr. Davis and cabinet, nor any other act not required by military necessity and in accordance with the usages of war."[52] Meade later wrote to his wife that as a matter of official duty he had to impugn the authenticity of the papers, but that "Kilpatrick's reputation, and collateral evidence in my possession, rather go against this theory."[53]

Most historians today accept the authenticity of the Dahlgren papers, but differ on who was responsible for the orders to kill Davis and the Confederate cabinet and burn Richmond.[54] David Herbert Donald is equivocal, noting that although the papers "could not be linked to Lincoln," the raid "did reflect the President's determination to take whatever steps were necessary to end the rebellion."[55] Edwin Fishel's history of military intelligence in the Army of Potomac attributes the papers to Dahlgren himself.[56] Stephen Sears and James O. Hall place the blame on everyone's favorite villain of Civil War Washington, Secretary of War Stanton.[57]

David Long argues forcefully that Lincoln may well have personally approved these plans, noting that Stanton was not likely to have made such an important decision without informing the president.[58] Indeed, only a week before Kilpatrick's visit to the White House, President Lincoln discovered that Secretary Stanton had authorized Bishop Edward Ames to take control of disloyal Methodist churches in the South, contrary to the president's often-expressed position of neutrality in church disputes.[59] So soon after the president had expressed displeasure over this fiasco, it does seem unlikely that Stanton would issue an even more controversial set of orders without at least consulting Lincoln.

The killing of Jefferson Davis and his cabinet should be distinguished from the capturing of them. The laws and usages of war recognized that the "chief officers of the hostile government, its diplomatic agents, and all persons who are of particular and singular use and benefit to the hostile army or its government" were subject to capture and could be held as prisoners of war.[60] As prisoners of war, however, their killing would be unlawful, except possibly as an act of retaliation for enemy violations.[61]

Capture of Davis and some or all of his cabinet would have given Lincoln legitimate leverage in resolving the dispute over the exchange of prisoners of war. By custom, higher-ranking officers were worth more for exchange purposes than private soldiers. During the War of 1812, for example, British and American military authorities agreed that a major general could be exchanged for thirty private soldiers, and a colonel for fifteen privates. The Dix-Hill Cartel concluded during the Civil War provided that a major general could be exchanged for forty privates, while a colonel was still worth fifteen privates.[62] Given this nineteenth-century mind-set, what would a captured president and several cabinet secretaries be worth? Perhaps they would be valuable enough for the Confederacy to agree that African American soldiers were prisoners of war. This underlines the importance of taking Davis and his cabinet alive, for exchange negotiations. Killing them would be not only unnecessary but also counterproductive.

David Long suggests two possible reasons Lincoln might nevertheless have approved the killing of Jefferson Davis. First, that the removal
of Davis would place Lincoln's old friend, Vice President Alexander
Stephens, in the Confederate White House, and that Stephens would
then be able to negotiate an acceptable end to the war. Second, that
killing him would have been a proper act of retaliation for Davis's policy
of enslaving African American soldiers and turning their white officers
over to state authorities to be prosecuted for inciting slave revolt.

President Lincoln could overcome his visceral aversion to killing reprisal prisoners if a military commander convincingly asserted a
military necessity to carry out the execution, as General Rosecrans did
in Missouri. Would Long's reasons be seen by Lincoln, or Stanton, as
evidence of a convincing military justification for retaliatory action, or
even violating the laws of war themselves? By 1864, there were two
conditions Lincoln viewed as essential to any negotiated peace arrangement—restoration of the Union and recognition of the Emancipation
Proclamation. There is no evidence that Alexander Stephens, who as
vice president had sworn to defend the Constitution of the Confederate
States, would have been more amenable to these conditions than Davis
had been.

Even if Stephens were so inclined, it is extremely unlikely he would
have had the political power to follow through. There would be no reason for Lincoln to think that, in the political atmosphere that would
have followed the assassination of Davis, Stephens would have been
allowed to negotiate a peace acceptable to him. Any negotiated peace
arrangement would presumably have had to be accepted by the Confederate Congress (which would thereby agree to put itself out of existence), the legislatures of the seceded states, and, most important, the
officers and men of the Confederate army. This is why Lincoln always
stressed to his generals that destroying Lee's army was more important
than capturing Richmond. As he argued in his public letter to James
Conkling, any peace agreement, "to be effective, must be made, either
with those who control the rebel army, or with the people first liberated
from the domination of that army, by the successes of our own army."
He explained: "I do not believe any compromise, embracing the maintenance of the Union, is now possible. All I learn, leads to a directly opposite belief. The strength of the rebellion, is its military—its army. That
army dominates all the country, and all the people, within its range. Any
offer of terms made by any man or men within that range, in opposition

to that army, is simply nothing for the present; because such man or men, have no power whatever to enforce their side of a compromise, if one were made with them."[63]

Being subjected to what is perceived as an unfair attack has generally made populations more belligerent rather than less. Most people in the North regarded the bombardment of Fort Sumter as unjustified, with the result that they rallied behind the Lincoln administration at the start of the Civil War. The assassination of Lincoln in 1865 certainly did not lead the people of the North to seek an easier peace for the defeated South. This was entirely predictable, and there was every reason to think that the people of the South would have reacted similarly to an assassination. For Lincoln to believe that the key to peace was to bring Stephens into office by killing Davis would require a great deal of wishful thinking on the president's part. Three years of brutal war had cured Lincoln of that.

By way of historical comparison, at the height of World War II, the British special operations executive developed a plan to assassinate Adolf Hitler. The plan was never approved by the British government, not because of legal or moral qualms, but because "from Churchill downwards there existed a widespread conviction that the elimination of Hitler would not be advantageous and [might] be positively counterproductive."[64] A successful assassination could even have produced "an intense rallying around the cult of the 'martyred' Führer" and increased determination to resist the Allies.[65] There is every reason to believe that as experienced statesmen, Lincoln and Stanton would have reached a similar conclusion if they ever seriously considered killing Jefferson Davis.

The theory that Davis would be assassinated specifically to bring Stephens into the Confederate presidency does not explain why President Lincoln would also have authorized the killing of Davis's cabinet and the burning of Richmond. The latter act, to be carried out by the freed prisoners of war, could only be considered a destructive act of revenge, with no military justification. Destruction or killing solely for revenge were things that Lincoln had always firmly opposed.

It is also difficult to see how Lincoln could have regarded the killing of Davis as a justified and prudent act of retaliation. For one thing, it is not clear what Confederate action he would be retaliating against in the middle of February 1864. Although Jefferson Davis had ordered that officers of African American units be delivered to state authorities for prosecution, this order had not yet been carried out. The U.S. government had received reports that captured soldiers had been enslaved or killed, but so far these were second-hand accounts that were hard to confirm.[66] African American soldiers were refused quarter at the battle of Olustee, Florida, on February 20, 1864, but this occurred after Colonel Kilpatrick's meeting with Lincoln and Stanton on February 13. The most notorious incidents in which African American soldiers were shot after surrendering happened much later in 1864. The battles of Fort Pillow, Tennessee, and Poison Spring, Arkansas, were fought in April, and the battle of Saltville, Virginia, in October. Lincoln's own Order of Retaliation, issued in response to Davis's proclamation, had threatened that "for every soldier of the United States killed in violation of the laws of war, a rebel soldier shall be executed."[67] It said nothing about killing in response to an implied threat to kill U.S. soldiers, which is all Davis had issued at the time the raid was planned.

Finally, there were sound foreign policy reasons not to carry out the acts called for in the Dahlgren papers. The British press was generally pro-Confederate, and was already carrying lurid accounts and cartoons of supposed Union atrocities.[68] The Confederate government quickly sent reproductions of the Dahlgren papers to its agents in Europe, who reproduced and distributed them to add to the anti-Union bonfire.[69] Carrying out the atrocities threatened in the papers would have raised anti-Union sentiment to a white heat, at the very time the United States was trying to persuade the British government to prevent more Confederate warships from being built or purchased in Great Britain.

The political and military disadvantages of killing Davis and burning Richmond clearly outweighed the insubstantial benefits, as both Lincoln and Stanton would have seen. This grandiose scheme does not sound like anything developed or approved by mature public officials. Instead, it sounds like something thought up on the spur of the moment by a young and daring officer who did not always exercise good judgment—that is, by Ulric Dahlgren. After consideration, Colonel Dahlgren himself probably gave up these ideas. All the survivors of his band of raiders insisted he had never actually told them to kill Davis or burn Richmond.

Conclusion

"Government Should Not Act for Revenge"

Under the standards of his time, President Lincoln did not authorize or condone any violations of the laws of war against enemy civilians. Beyond this generalization, the record suggests additional conclusions that may be drawn on Lincoln's policies toward Southern civilians and how those policies reflect his leadership style and personality.

As Union armies inexorably advanced into hostile areas, Southern civilians began to approach Abraham Lincoln for relief from military decisions. When Lincoln dealt with these petitions he concentrated on two issues—revenge and military necessity. Acts based on military necessity usually were legitimate. Acts of revenge never were. The government, Lincoln believed, "can properly have no motive of revenge, no purpose to punish merely for punishment's sake."[1] By forestalling acts of revenge, the president also reinforced one of the central concepts of the contemporary law of war. The Lieber Code repeatedly denounced revenge as an unlawful motive for military action.[2]

Often, revenge and military necessity were opposite sides of the same coin. An act of revenge or malice would be based on emotion, and one of the basest human emotions at that, not on rational military calculation or the "cold, calculating unimpassioned reason" that Lincoln regarded as the only sound basis for government policy.[3] "He glorified the operation of reason," Allen Guelzo has observed, "and shunned appeals to passion."[4]

In its essence, the principle of military necessity is the application of reason to the waging of war. The Lieber Code defined military necessity as "those measures which are indispensable for securing the ends of the war."[5] The words "necessity" and "indispensable" should not be taken literally. The code explained:

Military necessity admits of *all* direct destruction of life or limb of armed enemies, and of other persons whose destruction is incidentally unavoidable in the armed contests of the war; it allows of the capturing of every armed enemy, and every enemy of importance to the hostile government, or of peculiar danger to the captor; it allows of all destruction of property, and obstruction of the ways and channels of traffic, travel, or communication, and of all withholding of sustenance or means of life from the enemy; of the appropriation of whatever an enemy's country affords necessary for the subsistence and safety of the army, and of such deception as does not involve the breaking of good faith.[6]

What military necessity authorizes is hostile action that has a rational relationship to the defeat of the enemy's armed forces.

When defending the Emancipation Proclamation in the summer of 1863, Lincoln similarly defined military action as lawful if it "helps us, or hurts the enemy": "Is there—has there ever been—any question that by the law of war, property, both of enemies and friends, may be taken when needed? And is it not needed whenever taking it, helps us, or hurts the enemy? . . . Civilized belligerents do all in their power to help themselves, or hurt the enemy, except a few things regarded as barbarous or cruel. Among the exceptions are the massacre of vanquished foes, and non-combatants, male and female."[7] Lincoln also recognized that military necessity required that decisions be made even though all the consequences could not be foreseen. More than a year earlier, he had warned that war had its own logic and that it was "impossible to foresee all the incidents, which may attend and all the ruin which may follow it."[8]

His belief that military operations must be based on reason, and not on emotions such as malice or revenge, may explain Lincoln's refusal to pardon two Confederate officers convicted of conducting clandestine hostilities in the North. Captain Robert C. Kennedy, Confederate army, and Acting Master John Yates Beall, Confederate navy, were tried by the same military commission in New York City in January and February 1865. Both were sentenced to hang, and both appealed to President Lincoln for clemency.[9] Captain Kennedy was convicted of espionage and violation of the law of war. The latter charge was based on his participation in a Confederate operation that started fires in New York City on November 26, 1864.[10] It was this charge that probably sealed his fate in Lincoln's mind. The raid had originally been scheduled for election day, November 8, as part of an effort to frustrate Lincoln's re-election, but it had been put off when Union troops arrived to provide election security. Three weeks later, equipped with 144 bottles of an incendiary substance called Greek fire, the conspirators, dressed as civilians, set fire to nineteen hotels and P. T. Barnum's Museum in Manhattan.

President Lincoln himself had shown interest in developing incendiary artillery shells and had approved their use in the sieges of Charleston and Vicksburg. Nevertheless, in the president's mind there would have been important differences between those operations and Kennedy's. Charleston and Vicksburg were fortified cities under siege, and the bombardments were intended to speed their surrender. Union land and naval forces that could occupy the cities were close by. Use of incendiary shells in those circumstances arguably had an accepted military purpose.

There was no Confederate army near New York in November 1865 that could have occupied Manhattan if it surrendered. Neither did the raiders try to destroy the New York navy yard or any other legitimate military targets. Instead, they set fire to hotels and a popular tourist attraction, sites that would endanger the maximum number of civilian lives. (Captain Kennedy himself set fire to Barnum's Museum.) The attempt to burn Manhattan appeared to have no rational military purpose, and was therefore not justified by the principle of military necessity. To the president, it would have appeared to be nothing but an act of malice or revenge. No action was taken on Kennedy's petition and he was hanged on March 25, 1865.

Earlier in the war, Acting Master John Yates Beall had led a raid against a lighthouse on Virginia's Eastern Shore. Union authorities believed the raid had been carried out by local Confederate sympathizers, and a collective fine of $20,000 was assessed against the citizens of Northampton County. President Lincoln suspended the fine, but may have later reinstated it after local civilians boasted that the suspension was a victory over the federal government.[11]

After being captured and exchanged, Beall went to Canada to organize a clandestine mission to liberate Confederate prisoners of war held on Johnson's Island, Ohio. Posing as civilian passengers, on September 19, 1864, Beall and his team boarded the steamship *Philo Parsons* as she sailed her regular route on Lake Erie. They seized the steamship and another civilian vessel, scuttled the latter, put the passengers safely ashore, and sailed toward Johnson's Island. The mission was aborted when the *Philo Parsons* encountered the USS *Michigan* and Beall's crew refused to go farther. Beall sailed the *Philo Parsons* to neutral Canada. On December 16, Beall, in civilian clothes, was arrested in New York State after attempting to derail a passenger train the previous night. He was convicted of espionage and of violating the law of war as an unlawful belligerent.[12]

Unlike Kennedy, Beall attracted widespread sympathy in the North. Many, including Lincoln's old friend Orville Browning, appealed to the president for clemency on his behalf. Ninety-one members of Congress, including the Speaker of the House, petitioned the president to commute the sentence.[13] Congressman Thaddeus Stevens, a Radical Republican not otherwise known for pro-Confederate sympathies, asked Lincoln to at least postpone the execution for a month, "as a personal favor."[14] President Lincoln was unmoved, and Beall was executed on February 24, 1865.

Beall's most prominent offense, the attempt on Johnson's Island, at least had a rational military purpose. In the president's mind, what put the noose around Beall's neck was the charge of attempting to derail a passenger train at night, thereby endangering numerous civilians. Derailing a passenger train in upstate New York could not be justified as an act of military necessity and, like Kennedy's offense, must have appeared to be an act of malice or revenge.

In the course of granting or denying individual petitions, the president necessarily came to some general legal and policy conclusions: for example, that the government should not run churches, that civilians should not be exiled for their religious beliefs, that seizure of houses and furniture could only rarely be justified on military grounds, and that both sides should stop house burning as an act of retaliation. What is surprising to those familiar with the policy-making role of modern presidents is that he so rarely codified these positions into executive orders and sent them out as general guidance to all his field commanders and other concerned officials. Specific churches in St. Louis and Memphis were returned to their congregations, but even Lincoln's own secretary of war remained ignorant of Lincoln's policy on the military interfering with churches. Grant's order to expel "Jews as a class" was reversed, but no general warning was given to other department commanders. The provost marshal in Arkansas might return Mary Morton's house, but other provost marshals would not benefit from the president's guidance.

No order was issued to stop retaliatory house burning, despite General Grant's recommendation.

In other contexts, Abraham Lincoln enjoyed working with general principles from which specific, practical conclusions could be drawn. Judge David Davis and John Todd Stuart, who rode the Illinois Eighth Judicial Circuit with him, recalled that while other lawyers were reading novels and similar fare for amusement, Lincoln was studying Euclid's *Geometry*, which was based on deductive reasoning from a few definitions and axioms.[15] The intellectual foundation of Lincoln's opposition to slavery was in turn based on Euclidean reasoning from the general proposition that "all men are created equal" in the Declaration of Independence: "One would start with great confidence that he could convince any sane child that the simpler propositions of Euclid are true; but, nevertheless, he would fail, utterly, with one who should deny the definitions and axioms. The principles of Jefferson are the definitions and axioms of free society."[16] Lincoln, more than most American lawyers, long admired Blackstone's *Commentaries on the Laws of England* because that work reduced the chaos of common law judicial precedents to a coherent and orderly system of legal principles.[17] Nevertheless, although he seems to have enjoyed working with general principles himself, President Lincoln rarely offered his field commanders general guidance on the treatment of enemy civilians.

Instead of issuing general guidance, President Lincoln tended to wait until specific abuses were brought to his attention by individual petitioners. Lincoln biographer Richard Carwardine noted a similar tendency in the president's handling of internal security issues in the North: "Once in place, . . . the Union's internal security system operated routinely with little input for the president. His interventions in individual cases, whether to exercise mercy or prevent injustice, operated only at the margins, as military justice became a valued and potent buttress to the Union cause."[18] Lincoln's law partner William Herndon also noticed this aspect of his personality, and attributed it to a lack of imagination. In Herndon's opinion, Lincoln had difficulty imagining suffering in the abstract; he had to be presented with a concrete example before his humane impulses were engaged: "Mr Lincoln was tender hearted when in the presence of suffering or when it was enthusiastically or poetically described to him[;] he had great charity for the weaknesses of his fellow man[;] his nature was merciful and it sprang into manifestation quickly on the presentation of a proper subject under proper conditions[,] [but] he had no imagination to invoke, through the distances, suffering, nor the fancy to paint it. The subject of mercy must be presented to him."[19]

Herndon, however, is not necessarily a reliable authority on Abraham Lincoln's powers of imagination. After the Lincolns visited Niagara Falls, Herndon asked his partner for his reaction. "The thing that struck me most forcibly," Lincoln replied, "was, where in the world did all that water come from?" Herndon believed this answer demonstrated the pedestrian character of Abraham Lincoln's mind; he simply lacked the mental ability to appreciate the "magnificence and grandeur of the scene."[20]

Herndon was unaware of the unpublished essay Lincoln had written on the Falls. There, Lincoln observed that Niagara Falls' "power to excite reflection, and emotion, is [its] great charm." His own reflections concluded that, based on the Falls' erosion back from Lake Ontario, a geologist could demonstrate that the earth was at least 25,000 years old. Estimating that 500,000 tons of water went over Niagara Falls each minute, and reflecting that all of it had previously been lifted to the sky by evaporation, Lincoln was "overwhelmed in the contemplation of the vast power the sun is constantly exerting in [the] quiet, noiseless operation of lifting water *up* to be rained *down* again."[21] Abraham Lincoln may have lacked romantic imagination, but he definitely had a rational imagination. Conceiving and drafting prudent military guidance on the treatment of civilians required the latter, not the former.

We know he was capable of using his powers as commander in chief to issue general policies for the armed forces because he did it several times. Most notably, the 1863 Emancipation Proclamation told the army and navy how to treat refugees from slavery. Earlier, his orders of July 22, 1862, provided general guidance on the use and seizure of civilian property for military purposes. These, however, were exceptions. He considered issuing other general rules and then, for whatever reason, did not follow through. He drafted a proposal to allow wives and children to join men exiled to the Confederacy, but never sent it to Secretary Stanton.[22] His letter to General Reynolds on the seizure of Mary Morton's house included general legal and policy guidance on the treatment of civilian property. As we have seen, he also proposed a military-to-military agreement to stop retaliatory house burning.

One reason the president did not reissue his decisions in individual cases as general directives may lie in his reluctance to embarrass his subordinates. Lincoln was always reluctant, as he liked to put it, to plant "a thorn in any man's bosom."[23] For example, most students of Lincoln are familiar with his practice of writing critical letters to individuals who had displeased him and never sending them to the intended recipient out of concern for that person's feelings and reaction.[24] When the president wrote to John Hogan, who had complained about Secretary Stanton's order placing a loyal Methodist bishop in charge of disloyal churches in the South, that "it is not quite easy to withdraw it entirely, and at once," his reluctance probably stemmed from a desire not to embarrass either Stanton or the bishop.[25] Similarly, publishing a general order that persons should not be exiled from military departments solely on the basis of religion would have embarrassed General Grant, the only commander to have issued such an order.

A preference for deciding specific cases rather than issuing general proclamations would also have been consistent with Lincoln's experience as a lawyer. The law of Illinois, like the law of all the United States except Louisiana, was based on the English common law. Under a common law system, judges' decisions in individual cases, based on specific factual situations, serve as precedents to be followed in similar situations in the future. As more and more cases are decided applying a precedent, or deciding that the precedent did not apply to a new set of facts, the legal principles underlying the decisions are gradually fleshed out. Lincoln admired Blackstone's *Commentaries* for bringing order and coherence to this intimidating mass of judicial precedents, but as a practicing lawyer Lincoln had to function within this incremental process of law making. He described the process in one of his critiques of the U.S. Supreme Court's *Dred Scott* decision:

Judicial decisions have two uses—first to absolutely determine the case decided, and secondly, to indicate to the public how other similar cases will be decided when they arise. For the latter use, they are called "precedents" and "authorities." . . .

Judicial decisions are of greater or lesser authority as precedents, according to circumstances. . . . If this important decision had been made by the unanimous concurrence of the judges, and without any apparent partisan bias, and in accordance with legal public expectation, and with the steady practice of the departments [of the federal government] throughout our history, and had been, in no part, based on assumed historical facts which are not really true; or, if wanting in some of these, it had been before the court more than once, and had there been af-firmed and re-affirmed through a course of years, then it might be . . . factious . . . not to acquiesce in it as a precedent.[26]

Lincoln's point, of course, was that the *Dred Scott* decision lacked all of the qualities that would make a judicial decision respected and followed in a common law system.

As president, Lincoln applied this common law approach to deci-sion making when asked to rule on whether certain Missouri militia units were "State troops" or "United States troops." The president wrote to Attorney General Edward Bates that he would not answer the ques-tion in the abstract, but, like a common law judge, only in response to a concrete problem, so that he knew what the consequences of his answer would be: "I . . . think it safer when a practical question arises, to decide that question directly, and not indirectly, by deciding a general abstrac-tion supposed to include it, and also including a great deal more."[27] Based on his familiarity with common law legal methods, the president may similarly have preferred to develop his policies toward Southern civilians on a case-by-case basis, rather than by issuing general orders to his commanders in the field.

More fundamental philosophical and psychological factors were at work as well. It is well documented that Abraham Lincoln believed that the most important issues in life were decided by forces beyond anyone's control. An early reflection of this belief appears in an 1842 letter to his best friend, Joshua Speed, then a newlywed. In reply to expressions of gratitude for Lincoln's role in helping Speed overcome his doubts about marriage, Lincoln wrote that he regarded the match as "fore-ordained," and that he believed "God made me one of the instruments of bringing you and your Fanny together."[28] "I claim not to have controlled events," he wrote twenty-two years later as president, "but confess plainly that events have controlled me. Now, at the end of three years struggle the nation's condition is not what either party, or any man devised, or ex-pected. God alone can claim it."[29] "What is to be will be and no care of ours can arrest the decree" was Lincoln's "maxim and philosophy" ac-cording to his widow.[30] According to his political and professional col-league Leonard Swett, "he believed the results to which certain causes tended, would surely follow; he did not believe that those results could be materially hastened, or impeded."[31]

The president's reluctance to initiate general rules limiting his army's treatment of enemy civilians would be consistent with his well-attested belief that his life was ultimately ruled by forces beyond his control. David Herbert Donald has attributed this attitude to fatalism and an essentially "passive" nature.[32] Allen Guelzo and Ronald White, in contrast, have attributed it to a growing belief in the providence of God, who controlled events on earth.[33] Lucas Morel has also observed that classifying Lincoln as merely a fatalist "suggests a deistic view of the world that contradicts Lincoln's belief that God directed the affairs of men not only through impersonal laws and forces but also in response to their prayers and through their very actions."[34]

Whatever the philosophical basis of this belief, it would necessarily discourage any effort to control the treatment of enemy civilians by means of general orders or regulations. If Providence or fate had decreed that certain individuals should suffer, even unjustly, it would be futile for the president to try to prevent it. Lincoln's experiences in the first year of his administration would have reinforced the belief that laying down general military guidelines would be an exercise in futility. His declaration of April 19, 1861, that Confederate privateers would be treated as pirates ended in a humiliating retreat by the administration in January 1862. On January 27, 1862, the president issued his "General War Order No. 1," requiring all land and naval forces to advance simultaneously on February 22.[35] On January 31, he issued "Special War Order No. 1," requiring the Army of the Potomac to advance against Manassas, Virginia, on February 22.[36] Both orders appeared to be futile, since neither was obeyed.

On some issues, particularly slavery, Lincoln believed, or hoped, that Providence would make him an instrument of the divine will.[37] Similarly, when specific instances of injustice or cruelty had been brought to the president's attention, it would appear that Providence had placed these cases before him, and Lincoln could feel free to express his personal humanitarian tendencies.

In the end, Abraham Lincoln may have been reluctant to issue general guidelines for the treatment of Southern civilians for the same reason he was reluctant to join the abolitionists. Even when dealing with an evil as great as slavery, he was doubtful of his ability to predict and control all the consequences of sweeping reforms. In 1854, at the beginning of his campaign to reverse the Kansas-Nebraska Act, he readily admitted that he did not know the best way to abolish slavery where it already existed: "If all earthly power were given me, I should not know what to do, as to the existing institution."[38] He issued the Emancipation Proclamation only after more than a year of unsuccessful war convinced him that it was the will of Providence that he strike at slavery with the war power.[39]

To preserve the Union, Abraham Lincoln could tolerate such abominations as the Fugitive Slave Act of 1850 because he was convinced that slavery was "in the course of ultimate extinction" in the United States.[40] To restore the Union, President Lincoln would tolerate strong measures that brought injustice to some white civilians because he was convinced that these measures placed the rebellion on the course of ultimate defeat.

Notes

Introduction

1. Lincoln to Winfield Scott, April 25, 1861, *Collected Works of Abraham Lincoln* (hereafter cited as *Collected Works*), vol. 4, 344 (R. P. Basler ed. 1953).

2. See Michael Burlingame, *Abraham Lincoln: The Observations of John G. Nicolay and John Hay*, 51–55 (2007).

3. See Confederate States Army General Order 111, December 23, 1862, *War of the Rebellion: A Compilation of the Official Records of the Union and Confederate Armies* (hereafter cited as *Official Records*), series 1, vol. 15, 906; Howard Jones, "History and Mythology: The Crisis over British Intervention in the Civil War," in *The Union, the Confederacy and the Atlantic Rim*, 29, 43–45 (Robert May ed. 1995).

4. See, for example, Thomas DeLorenzo, *The Real Lincoln*, 171–99 (2002). When a statue of Lincoln was unveiled in Richmond, Virginia, in April 2003, protesters carried signs labeling him a "war criminal" (author's personal observation). For similar charges from an earlier generation of anti-Lincoln writers, see Dan Monroe, "Lincoln the Dwarf: Lyon Gardiner Tyler's War on the Mythical Lincoln," 24 *Journal of the Abraham Lincoln Association*, 32, 35 (2003), and Matthew Norman, "An Illinois Iconoclast: Edgar Lee Masters and the Anti-Lincoln Tradition," ibid. at 43, 51–52.

5. Noel Harrison, "Atop an Anvil: The Civilians' War in Fairfax and Alexandria Counties, April 1861–April 1862," 106 *Virginia Magazine of History and Biography*, 133, 135 (1998).

6. See Stephen W. Sears, *To the Gates of Richmond: The Peninsula Campaign*, 258 (1992).

7. Charles V. Mauro, *The Civil War in Fairfax County: Soldiers and Civilians*, 43 (2006).

8. Ibid., 33.

9. Robert E. Lee to Jefferson Davis, September 22, 1862, *Official Records*, series 1, vol. 19, part 2, 617–18.

10. Headquarters Army of Northern Virginia, September 22, 1862, to Generals James Longstreet and Thomas Jackson, *Official Records*, series 1, vol. 19, part 2, 618.

11. Michael G. Mahon, *The Shenandoah Valley 1861–1865*, 69–72 (1999).

12. General Order 71, Headquarters Army of Northern Virginia, December 12, 1864, in *The Civil War Archive: The History of the Civil War in Documents*, 372 (rev. ed., Henry Commager and Erik Bruun eds. 2000).

13. John M. Botts to John B. Fry, January 22, 1864, in "Mr. Lincoln's Virtual Library," the online collection of Lincoln papers at the Library of Congress (LOC), available at http://lcweb2.loc.gov/ammem/alhtml/alhome.html (hereafter cited as LOC Virtual Library).

14. See Thomas Lowry, *Tarnished Eagles: The Courts-Martial of Fifty Union Colonels and Lieutenant Colonels*, 87–89, 136–40 (1997).

15. Diary of Sarah Morgan, entry for August 13, 1862, in *The Civil War Archive*, 360–62 (Commager and Bruun eds.).

16. See, for example, Doris J. Janes, U.S. Department of Justice, Office of Justice Statistics, *Special Report: Profile of Jail Inmates, 2002* (July 2004).

17. Lee Kennett, *Marching through Georgia*, 287 (Harper Perennial paperback ed. 1996).

18. Address to the Young Men's Lyceum of Springfield, Illinois, January 27, 1838, *Collected Works*, vol. 1, 108, 115.

1. "With the Law of War in Time of War"

The chapter title quotation is from Lincoln to Conkling, August 26, 1863, *Collected Works*, vol. 6, 406, 408. Parts of this chapter were previously published in Burrus M. Carnahan, *Act of Justice: Lincoln's Emancipation Proclamation and the Law of War* (2007).

1. See David Herbert Donald, *Lincoln*, 302–3 (1995).

2. For example, Thaddeus Stevens, in *Recollected Words of Abraham Lincoln*, 423 (D. Fehrenbacher and V. Fehrenbacher eds. 1996).

3. Article 3, section 3.

4. Proclamation Calling Forth Militia and Convening Congress, April 15, 1861, *Collected Works*, vol. 4, 331–32.

5. Ibid. (emphasis added).

6. Isham G. Harris to Simon Cameron, April 17, 1861, *Official Records*, series 3, volume 1, 81.

7. Isham G. Harris to Abraham Lincoln, April 29, 1861, Library of Congress Lincoln Papers, online edition, http://memory.loc.gov/ammem/alhtml/alhome.html.

8. Lincoln to Isham G. Harris, May [1?] 1861, *Collected Works*, vol. 4, 351. The president's suspicions of Governor Harris were justified. Tennessee seceded and joined the Confederacy under Harris's leadership, and Harris fled the state when Nashville was occupied by U.S. forces in early 1862. He was serving as an aide to Confederate general Albert Sidney Johnson when the latter was killed at the battle of Shiloh.

9. 54 U.S. 115 (1851).

10. Doniphan's campaign is described in K. Jack Bauer, *The Mexican War*, 151–58 (1974).

11. 54 U.S. at 134.

12. Blockade Proclamation, April 19, 1861, *Collected Works*, vol. 4, 338–39.

13. See, for example, J. L. Brierly, *The Law of Nations*, 141 (6th ed. 1963).

14. See Dean B. Mahin, *One War at a Time*, 50–52 (1999).

15. For a popular history of this practice, see Donald A. Petrie, *The Prize Game: Lawful Looting on the High Seas in the Days of Fighting Sail* (1999).

16. See generally William Morrison Robinson Jr., *The Confederate Privateers* (1928; University of South Carolina paperback ed. 1994).

17. Meigs to Cameron, July 12, 1861, *Official Records*, series 2, vol. 3, 8.

18. McClellan to Assistant Adjutant General E. D. Townsend, July 13, 1861, *Official Records*, series 2, vol. 3, 9.

19. Scott to McClellan, July 14, 1861, *Official Records*, series 2, vol. 3, 10–11.

20. Seward to the president, August 2, 1861, *Official Records*, series 2, vol. 2, 37; General John Dix to General Wool, August 22, 1861, *Official Records*, series 2, vol. 3, 27–28.

21. *Inside Lincoln's Cabinet: The Civil War Diaries of Salmon P. Chase*, 49 (D. H. Donald ed. 1954).

22. General Grant to General Polk, October 14, 1861, *Official Records*, series 2, vol. 1, 511.

23. General Smith to General Gideon Pillow, November 26, 1861, *Official Records*, series 2, vol. 1, 523.

24. See, for example, Adjutant General Thomas to General Wool, November 29, 1861, *Official Records*, series 2, vol. 3, 148.

25. See, for example, Special Order 170, Headquarters U.S. Army, October 12, 1861, *Official Records*, series 2, vol. 3, 51–52 (57 Confederate prisoners to be released following Confederate release of 57 U.S. prisoners).

26. See, for example, Governor William Sprague (R.I.) to Lincoln, October 3, 1861; Governor John Andrew (Mass.) to Lincoln, November 25, 1861, LOC Virtual Library; *Inside Lincoln's Cabinet: The Civil War Diaries of Salmon P. Chase*, 49 (Donald ed.).

27. Joint Resolution adopted by the House of Representatives, December 11, 1861, *Official Records*, series 2, vol. 3, 157.

28. General Huger to Colonel Justin Dimick, January 20, 1862, *Official Records*, series 2, vol. 3, 199.

29. General Wool to Adjutant General Thomas, January 24, 1861, *Official Records*, series 2, vol. 3, 212.

30. Edwin Stanton to General Wool, February 11, 1862, *Official Records*, series 2, vol. 3, 254.

31. Wool to Stanton, February 23, 1862, *Official Records*, series 2, vol. 3, 301–8.

32. Stanton to Wool, February 26, 1862, *Official Records*, series 2, vol. 3, 322.

33. Cobb to Wool, February 28, 1862, *Official Records*, series 2, vol. 3, 338–39.

34. 12 U.S. (8 Cranch) 109 (1814).

35. 12 U.S. at 121 (emphasis added).

36. 54 U.S. 115 (1851).

37. *Brown v. United States*, 12 U.S. (8 Cranch) 110, 145 (1814) (Story, J., dissenting).

38. 12 U.S. at 152.

39. "He [the president] can exercise the rights which the state-of-war accords the United States under international law in regard to the enemy as well as to neutrals." Louis Henkin, *Foreign Affairs and the Constitution*, 52, 305 (n. 36) (1972).

40. *Luther v. Borden*, 48 U.S. (7 Howard) 1, 45 (1849) (emphasis added).

41. 54 U.S. 115 (1851).

42. The Prize Cases, 67 U.S. 635 (1863).

43. 67 U.S. at 688–89, 693.

44. 67 U.S. at 670 (emphasis original).

45. See Brian McGinty, *Lincoln and the Court*, 194–95 (2008).

46. Lincoln to Conkling, August 26, 1863, *Collected Works*, vol. 6, 406, 408.

47. See "Army, Union," in *The Civil War Society's Encyclopedia of the Civil War*, 16 (1997).

48. See Harold Hyman, *A More Perfect Union: The Impact of the Civil War and Reconstruction on the Constitution*, 147–50 (Sentry ed. 1975).

49. General Pope to Colonel Hurlbut, August 17, 1861, *Official Records*, series 2, vol. 1, 212.

50. Proclamation, Headquarters Department of the West, August 30, 1861, *Official Records*, series 2, vol. 1, 221.

51. General Frémont to Colonel Taylor, September 14, 1861, *Official Records*, series 2, vol. 1, 226.

52. General Order 1, Headquarters Department of the Missouri, St. Louis, January 1, 1862, *Official Records*, series 2, vol. 1, 247–49.

53. Instructions for the Government of Armies of the United States in the Field, General Order 100, War Department, Adjutant General's Office, April 24, 1863, *Official Records*, series 3, vol. 3, 148 (hereafter cited as Lieber Code). The Lieber Code is also in Dietrich Schindler and Jiri Toman, *The Laws of Armed Conflicts: A Collection of Conventions, Resolutions and Other Documents*, 6 *et seq.* (2nd ed. 1981) (hereafter cited as Schindler and Toman, *Laws of Armed Conflicts*).

54. Halleck to Schofield, May 22, 1863, *Official Records*, series 1, vol. 22, part 2, 291–92.

55. The full text of Lieber Code article 5 reads as follows: "Martial Law should be less stringent in places and countries fully occupied and fairly conquered. Much greater severity may be exercised in places or regions where actual hostilities exist, or are expected and must be prepared for. Its most complete sway is allowed—even in the commander's own country—when face to face with the enemy, because of the absolute necessities of the case, and of the paramount duty to defend the country against invasion./ To save the country is paramount to all other considerations."

56. Lieber Code, articles 14 and 15.

57. See Report of the United States Agent, *Papers Relating to the Treaty of Washington*, vol. 6, 52–55 (1874).

58. See Julius Stone, *Legal Controls of International Conflict*, 587 (1954).

59. Eritrea-Ethiopia Claims Commission, Partial Award, Western Front, Aerial Bombardment and Related Claims, Eritrea's Claim 25, Aerial Bombardment of Hirgigo Power Station, para. 117, rendered at The Hague, Netherlands, December 19, 2005.

60. See generally Burrus M. Carnahan, *Act of Justice: Lincoln's Emancipation Proclamation and the Law of War* (2007).

61. Lieber Code, article 16.

2. "Property, Both of Enemies and Friends, May Be Taken When Needed"

The chapter title quotation is from Lincoln to Conkling, August 26, 1863, *Collected Works*, vol. 6, 408.

1. Proclamation Calling Forth Militia and Convening Congress, April 15, 1861, *Collected Works*, vol. 4, 331.

2. See General P. G. T. Beauregard, "To the good People of the Counties of Loudoun, Fairfax, and Prince William," Headquarters Department of Alexandria [Virginia], June 5, 1861, *Official Records*, series 1, vol. 2, 907; William Lee Miller, *President Lincoln: The Duty of a Statesman*, 351–52 (2008).

3. Lincoln to Browning, September 22, 1861, *Collected Works*, vol. 4, 531.

4. Conversation with Hon. O. H. Browning at Leland Hotel Springfield June 17th 1875, in *An Oral History of Abraham Lincoln: John G. Nicolay's Interviews and Essays*, 1, 5 (Michael Burlingame ed. 1996).

5. See Richard Carwardine, *Lincoln: A Life of Purpose and Power*, 193–99 (2006).

6. See David Herbert Donald, *Lincoln*, 357–62 (1995).

7. See John C. Ropes, *The Army under Pope*, 1–18 (1881).

8. General Order 5, Headquarters Army of Virginia, July 18, 1862, *Official Records*, series 1, vol. 12, part 2, 50.

9. See General Pope to Lincoln, July 23, 1862, *Official Records*, series 1, vol. 12, part 3, 500–501; General Halleck to General McClellan, August 7, 1862, *Official Records*, series 1, vol. 11, part 3, 359.

10. *Inside Lincoln's Cabinet: The Civil War Diaries of Salmon P. Chase*, 95 (D. H. Donald ed. 1954).

11. *Collected Works*, Supplement 1832–1865, 141 (1974); published as General Order 109, War Department, Adjutant General's Office Washington, August 16, 1862, *Official Records*, series 3, vol. 2, 397.

12. *Inside Lincoln's Cabinet: The Civil War Diaries of Salmon P. Chase*, 95–96 (Donald ed.).

13. On the Lincoln administration's decision to apply the international laws of war in the Civil War, see Burrus M. Carnahan, *Act of Justice: Lincoln's Emancipation Proclamation and the Law of War*, 61–70 (2007).

14. Assistant Adjutant General R. H. Chilton to Lieutenant Colonel Turner Ashby, September 19, 1861, *Official Records*, series 1, vol. 5, 858; Michael Mahon, *The Shenandoah Valley, 1861–1865*, 38 (1999).

15. Secretary Judah Benjamin to General Johnston, December 27, 1861, *Official Records*, series 1, vol. 5, 1011.

16. Ulysses S. Grant, *Memoirs and Selected Letters*, 284 (Library of America ed. 1990).

17. Ibid., 291.

18. The U.S. Supreme Court adopted this doctrine during the War of 1812 in *United States v. Brown*, 12 U.S. (8 Cranch) 109 (1814). This was still the ruling precedent during the Civil War, and it was reaffirmed by the Court after the war in *Miller v. United States*, 78 U.S. 267, 313 (1870) and *Semmes v. United States*, 91 U.S. 21, 27 (1875).

19. Henry Wheaton, *Elements of International Law: With a Sketch of the History of the Science*, 252 (1836; Lawbook Exchange Ltd. facsimile reprint 2002).

20. See, for example, Gunther Rothenberg, "The Age of Napoleon," in *The Laws of War: Constraints on Warfare in the Western World*, 92–93 (Michael Howard, George Andreopoulos, and Mark Shulman eds. 1994); Clifford J. Rogers, "By Fire and Sword: *Bellum Hostile* and 'Civilians' in the Hundred Years War," in *Civilians in the Path of War*, 33, 61 (Mark Grimsley and Clifford J. Rogers eds. 2002).

21. "All pillage and sacking, even after taking a place by main force . . . are prohibited under the penalty of death, or such other severe punishment as may seem adequate for the gravity of the offense." Lieber Code, article 44. Some acts of pillage were punishable by court-martial under Articles of War 52 (a soldier who quits his "post or colors to plunder or pillage" may be punished with death or otherwise as a court-martial may direct) and 54 (committing

waste or spoil on property belonging to the U.S. citizens punishable as a court-martial may direct, but not with death). See *The 1863 Laws of War*, 15–16 (Stackpole Books 2005).

22. "The pillage of a town or place, even when taken by assault, is prohibited." Article 28, Regulations Respecting the Laws and Customs of War on Land Annexed to the 1899 Hague Convention with Respect to the Laws and Customs of War on Land, in Schindler and Toman, *Laws of Armed Conflicts*, 57, 78.

23. Elizabeth J. Beach to her parents, New Albany, Mississippi, July 29, 1864, in *The Civil War Archive: The History of the Civil War in Documents*, 363–64 (rev. ed., Henry Commager and Erik Bruun eds. 2000).

24. John A. Lynn, "A Brutal Necessity? The Devastation of the Palatinate, 1688–1689," in *Civilians in the Path of War*, 79, 94 (Grimsley and Rogers eds.).

25. General Order 287, Headquarters of the Army, National Palace of Mexico, September 17, 1847, reprinted in Marcus J. Wright, *General Scott*, 232–34 (1894).

26. Wright, *General Scott*, 323–24.

27. See, Marc Leepson, *Desperate Engagement*, 60–61, 99–100 (paperback ed. 2007); Fritz Haselberger, *Confederate Retaliation: McCausland's 1864 Raid* (2000); B. Franklin Cooling, *Monocacy: The Battle That Saved Washington*, 28, 97–99 (1997); Edward Y. Goldsborough, *The Appeal of Frederick City, Maryland, to The Congress of the United States, For the Payment of Its Claim of $200,000 Paid as a Ransom to the Confederate Army, July 9, 1864* (1902; reprint n.d.).

28. Lieber Code, articles 15 and 38.

29. Lincoln to General Reynolds, January 20, 1865, *Collected Works*, vol. 8, 228–29.

30. See Report of the United States Agent, *Papers Relating to the Treaty of Washington*, vol. 6, 52–55 (1874). See also *United States v. Alexander*, 96 U.S. 915 (1865), holding that cotton bales were property aiding the Confederacy under a federal statute.

31. Address before the Young Men's Lyceum of Springfield, Illinois, January 27, 1838: "The Perpetuation of our Political Institutions," *Collected Works*, vol. 1, 108. See also Allen Guelzo, "A. Lincoln, Philosopher," in *Lincoln's America, 1809–1865*, 7 (Joseph Fornieri and Sarah Gabbard eds. 2008); Richard Carwardine, *Lincoln: A Life of Purpose and Power*, 48–49 (Knopf ed. 2006); David Herbert Donald, *Lincoln*, 80–83 (1995). See also Lincoln to Stanton, Draft, March 18, 1864, *Collected Works*, vol. 7, 254, 255 ("the government . . . can properly have no motive of revenge, no purpose to punish merely for punishment's sake").

32. Curtis to Lincoln, December 28, 1862, LOC Virtual Library.

33. Lincoln to Curtis, January 2, 1863, *Collected Works*, vol. 6, 33.

34. Curtis to Lincoln, April 3, 1863, LOC Virtual Library.

35. Lincoln to Oliver Filley, December 22, 1863, *Collected Works*, vol. 7, 85.

36. Memorandum about Churches, March 4, 1864, *Collected Works*, vol. 7, 223.

37. Memorandum on Memphis Church, May 13, 1864, *Collected Works*, vol. 7, 339.

38. Washburn to Lincoln, June 22, 1864, LOC Virtual Library.

39. See "Order concerning Bishop Ames" from Assistant Adjutant General E. D. Townsend, War Department, Washington, November 30, 1863, to the Generals Commanding the Departments of the Missouri, the Tennessee and the Gulf, LOC Virtual Library; see also Order, Headquarters Department of the Missouri, St. Louis, February 12, 1864, *Official Records*, series 1, vol. 34, part 2, 311.

40. See Carwardine, *Lincoln: A Life of Purpose and Power*, 277–78.

41. Lincoln to Stanton, February 11, 1864, *Collected Works*, vol. 7, 179–80.

42. Endorsement to Hogan, February 13, 1864, *Collected Works*, vol. 7, 182–83.

43. Lincoln to General Rosecrans, April 4, 1864, *Collected Works*, vol. 7, 283–84.

44. Lincoln to Grant, August 14, 1864, *Collected Works*, vol. 7, 493.

45. David J. Eicher, *The Longest Night: A Military History of the Civil War*, 557 (2001).

46. For a description of the institutions of parole and exchange, see Gerald J. Prokopowicz, "Word of Honor: The Parole Systems in the Civil War," 6, no. 4 *North and South*, 24 (May 2003).

47. "ART. 5. Each party upon the discharge of prisoners of the other party is authorized to discharge an equal number of their own officers or men from parole, furnishing at the same time to the other party a list of their prisoners discharged and of their own officers and men relieved from parole, thus enabling each party to relieve from parole such of their own officers and men as the party may choose. The lists thus mutually furnished will keep both parties advised of the true condition of the exchange of prisoners." Dix-Hill Cartel, July 22, 1862, *Official Records*, series 2, vol. 4, 266–67.

48. See General Johnston to Jefferson Davis, July 13, 1862; Davis to Johnston, July 14, 1862, *Official Records*, series 1, vol. 24, part 1, 201–2.

49. See, for example, William Ludlow, U.S. Agent of Exchange, to Robert Ould, C.S. Agent of Exchange, July 22, 1863, *Official Records*, series 2, vol. 6, 136–37. This was one of many disputes over the meaning and application of the cartel that contributed to its breakdown in 1863.

50. Note, *Collected Works*, vol. 7, 493.

3. "Strong Measures, Deemed Indispensible but Harsh at Best"

The chapter title quotation is from Lincoln to Drake and others, October 5, 1863, *Collected Works*, vol. 6, 500.

1. War Department: Office of the Chief of Staff, *Rules of Land Warfare* (War Department Document No. 467, issued April 25, 1914), para. 383 (Kessinger Publishing reprint 2007).

2. General Order 1, Headquarters Department of the Missouri, January 1, 1862, *Official Records*, series 2, vol. 2, 247, 249.

3. Lieber Code, articles 56 and 57.

4. Proclamation of a Blockade, April 19, 1861, *Collected Works*, vol. 4, 338.

5. *United States v. William Smith*, October 22, 1861 (U.S. District Court for the Eastern District of Pa.), *Official Records*, series 2, vol. 3, 58, 69.

6. Davis to Lincoln, July 6, 1861, *Official Records*, series 2, vol. 3, 5–6.

7. Lieber Code, article 82. Similarly, civilians in occupied territory who committed hostile acts against the occupying forces were not lawful combatants and were also subject to punishment: "If . . . the people of a country, or any portion of the same, already occupied by an army, rise against it, they are violators of the laws of war, and are not entitled to their protection." Lieber Code, article 52. Later treaties have loosened the requirement that armed groups be commissioned by a government in order to be lawful belligerents.

8. Benjamin to Colonel W. B. Wood, *Official Records*, series 1, vol. 7, 701; Richard Nelson Current, *Lincoln's Loyalists*, 38–39 (1992).

9. Price to Halleck, January 12, 1862, *Official Records*, series 2, vol. 1, 255–56; Halleck to Price, January 22, 1862, *Official Records*, 258–59.

10. Lieber Code, article 81.

11. See Jeffrey D. Wert, *Mosby's Rangers*, 70–71 (1990); James A. Ramage, *Grey Ghost: The Life of Col. John Singleton Mosby*, 105–6, 131–33 (1999). In practice, Mosby's men also looted a good deal of private property, but so did many regular troops.

12. General Order 1, Headquarters Department of the Missouri, St. Louis, January 1, 1862, *Official Records*, series 2, vol. 1, 247–49.

13. Grant to Sheridan, August 16, 1864, *Official Records*, series 1, vol. 43, part 1, 811.

14. Sheridan to Grant, August 17, 1864, and August 19, 1864, *Official Records*, series 1, vol. 43, part 1, 822, 841; Wert, *Mosby's Rangers*, 211–22. Ramage, *Grey Ghost*, 197–200, 211.

15. Mosby to Lee, October 29, 1864, *Official Records*, series 1, vol. 43, part 1, 909–10.

16. Wert, *Mosby's Rangers*, 244–50; Ramage, *Grey Ghost*, 212–15.

17. General Order 7, Headquarters Army of Virginia, Washington, July 10[?], 1862, *Official Records*, series 1, vol. 12, part 2, 51.

18. See Halleck to McClellan, August 2, 1862, *Official Records*, series 1, vol. 11, part 3, 359.

19. See John J. Hennessy, *Return to Bull Run*, 15–16, 21–22 (1993).

20. War Department: Office of the Chief of Staff, *Rules of Land Warfare* (War Department Document No. 467, issued April 25, 1914), para. 386 (Kessinger Publishing reprint 2007). It also cited in support two British experts on international law, Spaight and Oppenheim. See also Michael Howard, *The Franco-Prussian War*, 250–51 (university paperback ed. 1981).

21. See Gunther Rothenberg, "The Age of Napoleon," in *The Laws of War: Constraints on Warfare in the Western World*, 95 (Michael Howard, George Andreopoulos, and Mark Shulman eds. 1994).

22. Hennessy, *Return to Bull Run*, 16.

23. Proclamation, Headquarters Army of the Potomac, July 30, 1863, *Official Records*, series 1, vol. 27, part 3, 286–87.

24. See Ramage, *Grey Ghost*, 217 (1999).

25. Sheridan to Grant, October 7, 1864, *Official Records*, series 1, vol. 43, part 1, 30–31.

26. Philip Sheridan, *The Personal Memoirs of P. H. Sheridan*, 308 (1888; reprint 1992).

27. See John L. Heatwole, *The Burning: Sheridan in the Shenandoah Valley*, 89–105 (1998); Ramage, *Grey Ghost*, 209–10 (1999).

28. Report of Major General Hunter, Headquarters Department of West Virginia, Harper's Ferry, August 8, 1864, *Official Records*, series 1, vol. 37, part 1, 96, 97; see also Edward A. Miller Jr., *Lincoln's Abolitionist General: The Biography of David Hunter*, 193–95 (1997).

29. Diary of Sarah Morgan, entry for August 13, 1862, in *The Civil War Archive: The History of the Civil War in Documents*, 360 (rev. ed., Henry Commager and Erik Bruun eds. 2000).

30. Lieber Code, article 28.

31. Lieber Code, article 17.

32. General Order 11, Headquarters Army of Virginia, July 23, 1862, *Official Records*, series 1, vol. 12, part 2, 52.

33. Pope to Lincoln, July 23, 1862, *Official Records*, series 1, vol. 12, part 3, 500–501.

34. See Hennessy, *Return to Bull Run*, 17.

35. Mark E. Neely Jr., *The Fate of Liberty*, 78 (1991).

36. See Sherman to Hood, September 7, 1864, in *Sherman's Civil War: Selected Correspondence of William T. Sherman, 1860–1865*, 704 (Brooks Simpson and Jean Berlin eds. 1999); Sherman to Halleck, July 7, 1864, in ibid., 662; Mark Grimsley, *The Hard Hand of War: Union Military Policy towards Southern Civilians 1861–1865*, 186–90 (1995), notes that the population of Atlanta

had fallen to only 3,000 during the siege, and that 1,644 people were actually evacuated under Sherman's order.

37. Thomas Goodrich, *Black Flag: Guerrilla Warfare on the Western Border 1861–1865*, 100 (1995).

38. See Neely, *The Fate of Liberty*, 48–49; William Lee Miller, *President Lincoln: The Duty of a Statesman*, 136–37 (2008).

39. Goodrich, *Black Flag*, 94.

40. General Order 11, Headquarters District of the Border, Kansas City, Mo., August 25, 1863, *Official Records*, series 1, vol. 22, part 2, 473.

41. See Goodrich, *Black Flag*, 97–100; Michael Fellman, *Inside War: The Guerrilla Conflict in Missouri during the American Civil War*, 95 (paperback ed. 1990).

42. Lincoln to Schofield, October 1, 1863, *Collected Works*, vol. 6, 492. See also John Hay's account of the original meeting: Memorandum, September 30, 1863, in *At Lincoln's Side: John Hay's Civil War Correspondence and Selected Writings*, 57–64 (Michael Burlingame ed. 2000).

43. To this day, international law places few restraints on the forcible military movement of civilian populations, if called for by military necessity. See Geneva Convention Relative to the Protection of Civilian Persons in Time of War, signed 12 August 1949 (Fourth Geneva Convention), article 49, in Schindler and Toman, *Laws of Armed Conflicts*, 427.

44. Report of Maj. Gen. Henry W. Halleck, U.S. Army, General-in-Chief, of operations in the Departments of the Missouri and of the Northwest, November 25, 1862–November 15, 1863, *Official Records*, series 1, vol. 22, part 1, 9, 11.

45. Lincoln to Stanton, September 1, 1863, *Collected Works*, vol. 6, 427.

46. Ibid.

47. General Order 11, Headquarters 13th Army Corps, Department of the Tennessee, Holly Springs, December 17, 1862, *Official Records*, series 1, vol. 17, part 2, 424.

48. See Halleck to Grant, January 4, 1863, *Official Records*, series 1, vol. 17, part 2, 530. See also Halleck to Grant, January 21, 1863, *Official Records*, series 1, vol. 24, part 1, 9 ("It may be proper to give you some explanation of the revocation of your order expelling all Jews from your department. The President has no objection to your expelling traitors and Jew peddlers, which, I suppose, was the object of your order; but, as it in terms proscribed an entire religious class, some of whom are fighting in our ranks, the President deemed it necessary to revoke it"); Doris Kearns Goodwin, *Team of Rivals*, 529 (2005).

49. Eliot A. Cohen, *Supreme Command*, 41 (2005).

50. See, for example, Lincoln to Curtis, January 5, 1863, urging leniency in the cases of John M. Robinson, James L. Matthews, and James L. Stephens, *Collected Works*, vol. 6, 36–37.

51. Drake to Lincoln, April 29, 1863, LOC Virtual Library.

52. Lincoln to Stanton, September 1, 1863, *Collected Works*, vol. 6, 427; Lincoln to Joseph Segar, September 5, 1863, and Note, *Collected Works*, vol. 6, 434.

53. Lincoln to J. R. Underwood and Henry Grider, Draft, October 26, 1864, *Collected Works*, vol. 8, 77–78.

54. See Eric Mills, *Chesapeake Bay in the Civil War*, 214 (1996).

55. General Order 6, Headquarters Department of the Cumberland, Chattanooga, Tenn., January 6, 1864, *Official Records*, series 1, vol. 32, part 2, 37–38.

56. See Goodrich, *Black Flag*, 128.

57. Samuel Lawrence to Henry Lockwood, December 2, 1864, *Official Records*, series 1, vol. 43, part 2, 728.

58. See Lowell H. Harrison, *The Civil War in Kentucky*, 76–77 (1975); Fellman, *Inside War*, 94–95; John F. Marszalek, *Commander of All Lincoln's Armies: A Life of Henry W. Halleck*, 110–11 (2004).

59. Lincoln to Stanton, September 1, 1863, *Collected Works*, vol. 6, 427.

60. Lincoln to Curtis, January 5, 1863, *Collected Works*, vol. 6, 36–37 (emphasis original).

61. Curtis to Lincoln, January 15, 1863, *Official Records*, series 1, vol. 22, part 2, 42.

62. Stanton to Curtis, January 20, 1863, *Official Records*, series 1, vol. 22, part 2, 64.

63. Lincoln to Boyle, February 1, 1863, *Collected Works*, vol. 6, 87.

64. See Lincoln to Underwood and Grider, Draft, October 26, 1864, *Collected Works*, vol. 8, 77.

65. Lincoln to Burbridge, October 27, 1864, *Collected Works*, vol. 8, 78.

66. See Harrison, *The Civil War in Kentucky*, 78.

67. Lowell H. Harrison, *Lincoln of Kentucky*, 194 (2000).

68. See, for example, Thomas Mays, *Cumberland Blood: Champ Ferguson's Civil War* (2008).

69. Harrison, *The Civil War in Kentucky*, 78.

70. See Harrison, ibid., 77; Marshall Myers, "Union General Stephen Gano Burbridge: The Most Hated Man in Kentucky," in *Kentucky's Civil War 1861–1865*, 144 (Jerlene Rose ed. 2005).

71. *The Hostages Case*, U.S. Military Tribunal, Nuremburg (1948), in *The Law of War: A Documentary History*, vol. 2, 1303, 1317 (Leon Friedman ed. 1972).

72. "Art. 33. No protected person may be punished for an offence he or she has not personally committed. Collective penalties and likewise all measures of intimidation or of terrorism are prohibited. . . . Reprisals against protected persons and their property are prohibited"; "Art. 34. The taking of hostages is

prohibited." Geneva Convention Relative to the Protection of Civilian Persons in Time of War, signed 12 August 1949 (Fourth Geneva Convention), in Schindler and Toman, *Laws of Armed Conflicts*, 427, 443.

73. See Note, *Collected Works*, vol. 6, 31; Mark Neely, *The Civil War and the Limits of Destruction*, 42–49 (2007). Neely assumes that there was no legal justification for McNeil's act; in fact, as noted above, execution of reprisal prisoners was an accepted practice in international warfare. The strongest argument for the illegality of the Palmyra killings is that they were disproportionate to the Confederate violation, that is, killing ten prisoners in retaliation for one kidnapped and presumably murdered civilian.

74. There are at least eleven petitions signed by more than 600 citizens from various localities in Missouri in support of McNeil in the LOC Virtual Library. McNeil's defense of his action to his commanding officer also made its way to the White House, McNeil to Curtis, December 24, 1862, LOC Virtual Library.

75. See Confederate States Army, General Order 111, December 23, 1862, *Official Records*, series 1, vol. 15, 906.

76. Order of Retaliation, July 30, 1863, *Collected Works*, vol. 6, 357.

77. Bates to Lincoln, May 4, 1864; Stanton to Lincoln, May 5, 1864, LOC Virtual Library.

78. Lincoln to Stanton, May 17, 1864, *Collected Works*, vol. 7, 345.

79. "Frederick Douglass," in *Reminiscences of Abraham Lincoln by Distinguished Men of His Time*, chapter 9, 185, 188–89 (1888; facsimile reprint ed. 1971).

80. Pierce Hawkins to Lincoln, January 29, 1865, LOC Virtual Library; see also Lincoln to Burbridge, February 2, 1865, *Collected Works*, vol. 8, 256.

81. See Barton Able and P. L. Terry to Lincoln, November 10, 1864; James Yeatman to Lincoln, November 10, 1864, LOC Virtual Library. The guerrilla leader, Colonel Timothy Reeves, a Baptist minister in civilian life, claimed that Wilson had never granted quarter to his men, and for that reason ordered Wilson shot after capture. Fellman, *Inside War*, 182. See also "Between Missourians: Civil War in Ripley County," *OzarksWatch*, online edition, http://thelibrary.org/lochist/periodicals/ozarkswatch/ow404i.htm (accessed August 1, 2009).

82. Lincoln to Rosecrans, November 10, 1864, *Collected Works*, vol. 8, 102.

83. Rosecrans to Lincoln, November 11, 1864, LOC Virtual Library.

84. Lincoln to Rosecrans, January 5, 1863, *Collected Works*, vol. 6, 39.

85. See T. Harry Williams, "The Military Leadership of North and South," in *Why the North Won the Civil War*, 38, 44–49 (paperback ed. David Herbert Donald ed., 2005).

86. Lincoln to Hooker, June 10, 1863, *Collected Works*, vol. 6, 257. Hooker, then in command of the Army of the Potomac, had suggested "a rapid advance on Richmond" following the battle of Brandy Station, Virginia.

87. Entries for October 19 and 25, 1863, in John Hay, *Inside Lincoln's White House: The Complete Civil War Diary of John Hay*, 94, 98–99 (Michael Burlingame and John Ettlinger eds. 1997).

88. Neely, *The Civil War and the Limits of Destruction*, 66.

89. Lincoln to Rosecrans, November 19, 1864, *Collected Works*, vol. 8, 116.

4. "War, at the Best, Is Terrible"

The chapter title quotation is from Speech at Philadelphia Sanitary Fair, June 16, 1864, *Collected Works*, vol. 7, 394.

1. Reports of MG John Pope, of the operations of the Army of Virginia, June 26–September 2, *Official Records*, series 1, vol. 12, part 2, 20, 23. Pope did not mention that the "want of supplies" in the countryside also impaired the retreat of his own army when the time came. See John J. Hennessy, *Return to Bull Run*, 53 (1993).

2. See, for example, John A. Lynn, "A Brutal Necessity? The Devastation of the Palatinate, 1688–1689," in *Civilians in the Path of War*, 88 (Mark Grimsley and Clifford Rogers eds. 2002); Russell F. Weigley, *The Age of Battles*, 109 (1991); Christopher Duffy, *The Military Experience in the Age of Reason, 1715–1789*, 302–3 (1987).

3. Emmerich de Vattel, *The Law of Nations, or the Principles of Natural Law*, book 3, chapter 9, paras. 166, "Waste and destruction," and 167, "Ravaging and burning" (1758; Joseph Chitty trans. 1797).

4. Adjutant and Inspector General S. Cooper to General Johnston, June 18, 1861, *Official Records*, series 1, vol. 2, 934–35.

5. Lieber Code, article 17.

6. See Geneva Convention Relative to the Protection of Civilian Persons in Time of War, signed 12 August 1949 (Fourth Geneva Convention), article 55, in Schindler and Toman, *Laws of Armed Conflicts*, 427, 459.

7. See Protocol I Additional to the Geneva Conventions of 12 August 1949, article 54, para. 1, in ibid., 551, 582.

8. Ulysses S. Grant, *Memoirs and Selected Letters*, 291 (Library of America 1990).

9. See, for example, Colonel William Philips to General Samuel Curtis, *Official Records*, series 1, vol. 22, part 2, 61; Stephen V. Ash, *When the Yankees Came*, 81–83 (1995).

10. Elizabeth J. Beach to her parents, New Albany, Mississippi, July 29, 1864, in *The Civil War Archive: The History of the Civil War in Documents*, 363–64 (rev. ed., Henry Commager and Erik Bruun eds. 2000) (emphasis original).

11. Ibid., 264.

12. See, for example, Lynn, "A Brutal Necessity?"; Weigley, *The Age of Battles*, 70.

13. *United States v. List and Others* (the Hostages Case), IX *Trials of War Criminal before the Nuremburg Military Tribunals*, 1296–97 (United States Military Tribunal 1948).

14. Lincoln to Stanton, July 22, 1862, *Collected Works*, Supplement 1832–1865, 141 (1974); also published as General Order 109, War Department, Adjutant General's Office, Washington, August 16, 1862, *Official Records*, series 3, vol. 2, 397.

15. General Halleck to General Hunter, July 17, 1864, *Official Records*, series 1, vol. 37, part 2, 366.

16. Grant also believed that the Shenandoah Valley was a major source of food for Lee's army defending the cities of Richmond and Petersburg, then under siege by Grant's forces. Ulysses S. Grant, *Memoirs and Selected Letters*, 614. See also Philip Sheridan, *The Personal Memoirs of P. H. Sheridan*, 265–66 (1888; reprint 1992). A recent study has cast doubt on this belief, pointing out that by the summer of 1864, the valley had little surplus food and forage left and Lee was actually obtaining most of his supplies by rail from Georgia. Michael G. Mahon, *The Shenandoah Valley 1861–1865*, 75, 102–3, 117–27 (1999). Mark Neely, *The Civil War and the Limits of Destruction* (2007), accepts some of Mahon's conclusions and argues (114) that the destruction, as actually carried out, was principally aimed at limiting the ability of Confederate forces to live off the land in the Valley.

17. See, for example, David Homer Bates, *Lincoln in the Telegraph Office*, 3, 88–91, 94–97, 113–23 (1907; reprint 1995). See generally Tom Wheeler, *Mr. Lincoln's T-Mails: How Abraham Lincoln Used the Telegraph to Win the Civil War* (2007).

18. Lincoln to Grant, August 3, 1864, *Collected Works*, vol. 7, 476, implies that Lincoln had been carefully following all telegraphic dispatches from the War Department: "I have seen your dispatch in which you say 'I want Sheridan put in command of all the troops in the field, with instructions to put himself south of the enemy, and follow him to the death. Wherever the enemy goes, let our troops go also.' This I think is exactly right, as to how our forces should move. But please look over the dispatches you may have received from here, even since you made that order, and discover, if you can, that there is any idea in the head of anyone here, of 'putting our army *South* of the enemy' or of following him to the 'death' in any direction. I repeat to you it will neither be done nor attempted unless you watch it every day, and hour, and force it." See also Lincoln to Grant, August 17, 1864, *Collected Works*, vol. 7, 499.

19. Edward A. Miller Jr., *Lincoln's Abolitionist General: The Biography of David Hunter*, 224 (1997).

20. Special Order 128, Headquarters Department of West Virginia, Harper's Ferry, W. Va., July 17, 1864, *Official Records*, vol. 37, part 2, 367.

21. Miller, *Lincoln's Abolitionist General*, 225–26; Fritz Haselberger, *Confed-*

erate Retaliation: McCausland's 1864 Raid, 63–66 (2000); Note, *Collected Works*, vol. 7, 446. Both men were distant relatives of General David Hunter.

22. Lincoln to Franklin Martindale, circa July 17, 1864, *Collected Works*, vol. 7, 445.

23. Haselberger, *Confederate Retaliation*, 66. Andrew Hunter was released from custody after a month. Ibid., 64.

24. Henrietta B. Lee to David Hunter, Shepherdstown, Virginia, July 20, 1864, in *The Civil War Archive: The History of the Civil War in Documents*, 365–66 (Commager and Bruun eds.).

25. Lieber Code, article 16.

26. See Miller, *Lincoln's Abolitionist General*, 226–27; Note, *Collected Works*, vol. 7, 477–78.

27. Endorsement to Edwin S. Stanton, August 3, 1864, *Collected Works*, vol. 7, 477.

28. Grant to Hunter, August 5, 1864, *Official Records*, series 1, vol. 43, part 1, 697–98.

29. Lincoln to Stanton, July 22, 1862, *Collected Works*, Supplement 1832–1865, 141 (1974); also published as General Order 109, War Department, Adjutant General's Office, Washington, August 16, 1862, *Official Records*, series 3, vol. 2, 397.

30. Grant to Sheridan, August 26,1864, *Official Records*, series 1, vol. 43, part 1, 916–17.

31. See Jeffrey D. Wert, *From Winchester to Cedar Creek: The Shenandoah Campaign of 1864*, 157–60 (1987).

32. See John L. Heatwole, *The Burning: Sheridan in the Shenandoah Valley* (1998): soldiers helping to prevent fires from spreading to private homes, 72–73, 137; one iron furnace spared burning because the workers' homes were too close to it, 74; widows' farms spared, 37, 40, 49, 51.

33. Ibid., 164.

34. See Sheridan to Grant, October 7, 1864, *Official Records*, series 1, vol. 43, part 1, 30–31. See also Heatwole, *The Burning*, 62, 130–31, 164.

35. See Mahon, *The Shenandoah Valley 1861–1865* and Neely, *The Civil War and the Limits of Destruction*.

36. Sheridan to Grant, September 24, 1864, *Official Records*, series 1, vol. 43, part 1, 28.

37. Sheridan to Grant, September 29, 1864, *Official Records*, series 1, vol. 43, part 1, 29–30.

38. Sheridan to Grant, October 7, 1864, *Official Records*, series 1, vol. 43, part 1, 30–31

39. General Custer to Major William Russell, November 15, 1864, *Official Records*, series 1, vol. 43, part 1, 529; General Wesley Merritt to Major Russell, October 5, 1864, *Official Records*, series 1, vol. 43, part 1, 442–43.

40. General Powell to Major Russell, October 27, 1864, *Official Records*, series 1, vol. 43, part 1, 508–11.

41. Vattel, *The Law of Nations, or the Principles of Natural Law*, book 3, chapter 9, paras. 166, "Waste and destruction," and 167, "Ravaging and burning."

42. In origin, these attitudes went back to the increasing professionalization of armies in the last quarter of the seventeenth century, and were reinforced by the experience of professionals in the Napoleonic Wars. See Weigley, *The Age of Battles*, 70–71, 541–43.

43. Sherman to the Hon. James Guthrie, August 14, 1864, in *Sherman's Civil War: Selected Correspondence of William T. Sherman, 1860–1865*, 693, 694 (Brooks Simpson and Jean Berlin eds. 1999). Sherman was responding to a complaint that General Stephen Burbridge, commanding the U.S. Military District of Kentucky, was needlessly arresting and exiling civilian citizens. "The rebels first introduced terror as part of their system," he went on, citing Confederate forced contributions during the Perryville campaign of 1862. "I will therefore sustain General Burbridge if satisfied he is not influenced by mere personal motives, and nothing has occurred to evince anything of the kind." Ibid., 695.

44. See Stanley P. Hirshorn, *The White Tecumseh*, 159 (1997).

45. Sherman to Grant, July 14, 1863, *Official Records*, series 1, vol. 24, part 2, 525–27.

46. Sherman to Grant, October 4, 1862, in *Official Records*, series 1, vol. 17, part 2, 259–62.

47. Sherman to Grant, first and second messages on July 21, 1863, *Official Records*, series 1, vol. 24, part 2, 530–31.

48. Victor David Hanson, *The Soul of Battle*, 172 (1999).

49. See Special Field Order 67, Headquarters Mil. Div. of the Mississippi, in the Field, Atlanta, Ga., September 8, 1864, *Official Records*, series 1, vol. 38, part 5, 837; Sherman to Hood, September 7, 1864, in *Sherman's Civil War*, 704 (Simpson and Berlin eds.).

50. Sherman to Hood, September 10, 1864, in *Sherman's Civil War*, 705–7 (Simpson and Berlin eds.); Sherman to James M. Calhoun et al., in ibid., 707–9.

51. William Tecumseh Sherman, *Memoirs*, 603 (1885; Library of America reprint, Charles Royster ed. 1990).

52. On October 11, 1864, Sherman had written Halleck that he valued his "opinion of matters of importance above those of any other, because I know you to be frank, honest, and learned in the great principles of history." *Official Records*, series 1, vol. 39, part 3, 203.

53. Sherman to Grant, October 11, 1864, *Official Records*, series 1, vol. 39, part 3, 202.

54. Stanton to Grant, October 12, 1864, *Official Records*, series 1, vol. 39, part 3, 222.

55. Grant to Sherman, October 12, 1864, *Official Records*, series 1, vol. 39, part 3, 222.

56. Grant to Stanton, October 13, 1864, *Official Records*, series 1, vol. 39, part 3, 239; Sherman to Thomas, October 20, 1864, *Official Records*, series 1, vol. 39, part 3, 377–78; see also Noah Andre Trudeau, *Southern Storm: Sherman's March to the Sea*, 41, 70 (2008).

57. Sherman to Thomas, October 20, 1864, *Official Records*, series 1, vol. 39, part 3, 378.

58. Special Field Order 120, Headquarters Mil. Div. of the Miss., in the Field, Kingston, Ga., November 9, 1864, paras. 4 and 6, *Official Records*, series 1, vol. 39, part 3, 713–14.

59. See Trudeau, *Southern Storm*, 51–52, 538.

60. See Lee Kennett, *Marching through Georgia*, 279 (Harper Perennial paperback ed. 1996); Trudeau, *Southern Storm*, 324–26.

61. Special Field Order 120, Headquarters Mil. Div. of the Miss., in the Field, Kingston, Ga., November 9, 1864, para. 5, *Official Records*, series 1, vol. 39, part 3, 713–14.

62. Sherman, *Memoirs*, 667. Kennett, *Marching through Georgia*, 275 claims that Sherman also ordered the burning of the Sandersville courthouse, and came close to ordering the destruction of the town; see also Trudeau, *Southern Storm*, 260–62.

63. Sherman to Lincoln, September 17, 1864 (telegram concerning political situation in Georgia), LOC Virtual Library (emphasis added).

64. See, for example, Landon Y. Jones, *William Clark and the Shaping of the West*, 310–15 (2004); Kerry A. Trask, *Black Hawk*, 141 *et seq.* (2006).

65. See Rodney O. Davis, *"Success . . . which Gave Him So Much Satisfaction": Lincoln in the Black Hawk War* (Historical Bulletin No. 52, Lincoln Fellowship of Wisconsin 1995); Kenneth J. Winkle, *The Young Eagle*, 86–93 (2001).

66. Winkle, *The Young Eagle*, 92–93.

67. Quoted in Trask, *Black Hawk*, 243.

68. Benjamin F. Irwin to William Herndon, September 22, 1866, in *Herndon's Informants*, 353 (Douglas L. Wilson and Rodney O. Davis 1998).

69. Trask, *Black Hawk*, 102–3, 243, 265.

70. George M. Harrison to William Herndon, January 29, 1867, in *Herndon's Informants*, 554–55 (Wilson and Davis).

71. See Joseph W. Danielson, "John Basil Turchin," in Encyclopedia of Alabama, http://www.encyclopediaofalabama.org/face/Article.jsp?id=h-1652 (accessed November 28, 2008).

72. See George C. Bradley and Richard L. Dahlen, *From Conciliation to Conquest: The Sack of Athens and the Court-Martial of Colonel John B. Turchin,*

109–21 (2006); Christopher B. Paysinger, "Sack of Athens," in Encyclopedia of Alabama, http://www.encyclopediaofalabama.org/face/Article.jsp?id=h-1819 (accessed November 28, 2008).

73. Bradley and Dahlen, *From Conciliation to Conquest*, 156–74, 201–20.

74. "The Court-Martial of Col. Turchin," *New York Times*, August 11, 1862, 2.

75. See Bradley and Dahlen, *From Conciliation to Conquest*, 222–26.

76. See Lincoln to Stanton, September 5, 1862, *Collected Works*, vol. 5, 406.

77. See Bradley and Dahlen, *From Conciliation to Conquest*, 6–8; Paysinger, "Sack of Athens."

78. See Bradley and Dahlen, *From Conciliation to Conquest*, 121, 270, note 11.

79. See generally Richard Lael, *The Yamashita Precedent: War Crimes and Command Responsibility* (1982).

80. Convention (II) Respecting the Laws and Customs of War on Land, 29 July 1899, article 1, in Schindler and Toman, *Laws of Armed Conflicts*, 65.

81. Protocol I Additional to the Geneva Conventions of 12 August 1949, article 86, para. 2, in ibid., 551, 602.

5. "Can You Get Near Enough to Throw Shells into the City?"

The chapter title quotation is from Lincoln to McClellan, May 26, 1862, *Collected Works*, vol. 5, 239–40.

1. Lincoln to Scott, April 25, 1861, *Collected Works*, vol. 4, 344. The draft in the LOC Virtual Library shows that the president initially wrote "suspicion" when he meant "suspension."

2. Michael Burlingame, *Abraham Lincoln: The Observations of John G. Nicolay and John Hay*, 69 (2007). See also Mark E. Neely Jr., *The Fate of Liberty*, 6–7 (1991).

3. Winfield Scott, *Memoirs of Lieut.-General Scott*, vol. 2, 427 (1864).

4. See John Eisenhower, *Agent of Destiny: The Life and Times of General Winfield Scott*, 240–44 (1997); K. Jack Bauer, *The Mexican War, 1846–1848*, 249–52 (1974).

5. General McClellan to Mary Ellen McClellan, October 11, November 18, and August 16, 1861, in *The Civil War Papers of George B. McClellan*, 106, 136, 85 (Stephen Sears ed. 1989).

6. See generally Tom Wheeler, *Mr. Lincoln's T-Mails: How Abraham Lincoln Used the Telegraph to Win the Civil War* (2007).

7. Lincoln to McClellan, May 26, 1862, *Collected Works*, vol. 5, 239–40.

8. Reproduced in the Report of MG McClellan, March 17–September 2, 1862, *Official Records*, series 1, vol. 12, 32–33.

9. Memorandum for Consideration of His Excellency the President, August 2, 1861, in *The Civil War Papers of George B. McClellan*, 71, 72 (Stephen Sears ed.).

10. McClellan to Lincoln, July 7, 1862, in ibid, 344.

11. Jackson to McLaws, September 14, 1862, *Official Records*, series 1, vol. 19, part 2, 607.

12. See, for example, Change No. 1, 15 July 1976, paras. 40a and 41 to Department of the Army Field Manual 27-10, *The Law of Land Warfare* (July 1956); U.S. Department of the Air Force, Air Force Pamphlet 110–31, *International Law—The Conduct of Armed Conflict and Air Operations* (November 19, 1976), para. 5-3c; Jean-Marie Henckaerts and Louise Doswald-Beck, *Customary International Humanitarian Law*, vol. 1, 3, 46 (2005).

13. See for example, Gunther Rothenberg, "The Age of Napoleon," in *The Laws of War: Constraints on Warfare in the Western World*, 86, 92 (Michael Howard, George Andreopoulos, and Mark Shulman eds. 1994).

14. McClellan to Scott, May 7, 1861, in *The Civil War Papers of George B. McClellan*, 16 (Stephen Sears ed.).

15. See Arthur Nussbaum, *A Concise History of the Law of Nations*, 162 (rev. ed. 1954).

16. Emmerich de Vattel, *The Law of Nations, or the Principles of Natural Law*, book 3, chapter 9, para. 169, "Bombarding towns."

17. See Richard Current, *The Lincoln Nobody Knows*, 180–81 (paperback ed. 1963). See generally Robert V. Bruce, *Lincoln and the Tools of War*, 241–45 (1956). Lincoln's papers contain many references to the president's interest in incendiary shells. See, for example, Lorin Blodget et al. to Lincoln [with endorsement by Lincoln], March 23, 1863; William B. Thomas to Lincoln, March 31, 1863; Stephen V. Benet to James W. Ripley, April 10, 1863; Oliver S. Halsted Jr., to Lincoln, April 25, 1863, LOC Virtual Library.

18. See entry for October 25, 1863, in John Hay, *Inside Lincoln's White House: The Complete Civil War Diary of John Hay*, 99 (Michael Burlingame and John Ettlinger eds. 1997).

19. See Department of the Army Field Manual 27-10, *The Law of Land Warfare* (July 1956), para. 36: "The use of weapons which employ fire, such as tracer ammunition, flame throwers, napalm and other incendiary agents, against targets requiring their use is not violative of international law."

20. "It is prohibited in all circumstances to make any military objective located within a concentration of civilians the object of attack by air-delivered incendiary weapons." Protocol on Prohibitions or Restrictions on the Use of Incendiary Weapons (Protocol III), article 2, para. 2. Geneva, October 10, 1980, International Committee of the Red Cross Web site, www.icrc.org/ihl.nsf/FULL/515?OpenDocument (accessed July 31, 2009).

21. Lieber Code, articles 17 and 18.

22. War Department: Office of the Chief of Staff, *Rules of Land Warfare* (War Department Document No. 467, issued April 25, 1914), paras. 218, 222 (Kessinger Publishing reprint 2007).

23. *The High Command Case*, U.S. Military Tribunal, Nuremburg (1948), in *The Law of War: A Documentary History*, vol. 2, 1421, 1459–60 (Leon Friedman ed. 1972).

24. Geneva Convention Relative to the Protection of Civilian Persons in Time of War, signed 12 August 1949 (Fourth Geneva Convention), article 17, in Schindler and Toman, *Laws of Armed Conflicts*, 427, 439.

25. Department of the Army Field Manual 27-10, *The Law of Land Warfare* (July 1956), para. 44a.

26. Sherman to Hood, September 14, 1864, in *Sherman's Civil War: Selected Correspondence of William T. Sherman, 1860–1865*, 710–11 (Brooks Simpson and Jean Berlin eds. 1999).

27. During the Franco-Prussian War of the 1870s, both sides bombarded civilian areas of cities under siege. See Michael Howard, *The Franco-Prussian War*, 274 (Kehl, Germany, and Strasbourg, France), 355–63 (Paris) (university paperback ed. 1981). For practices in the early nineteenth century, see Rothenberg, "The Age of Napoleon," 86, 92.

28. For recent summaries of the debate from various points of view, see, for example, Charles Royster, *The Destructive War*, 355–59 (1991); Mark Grimsley, *The Hard Hand of War: Union Military Policy towards Southern Civilians 1861–1865*, 190–215 (1995); James McPherson, "The Hard Hand of War," in *This Mighty Scourge*, 123–29 (2007); Mark E. Neely Jr., *The Civil War and the Limits of Destruction*, 198–206 (2008); Noah Andre Trudeau, *Southern Storm: Sherman's March to the Sea*, 533–35 (2008).

29. Michael R. Bradley, "In the Crosshairs," 10, no. 5 *North and South*, 34–61 (March 2008) argues that the Union army did indeed target Southern civilians for killing. However, the examples he cites as evidence are uniformly instances of retaliation for what the U.S. authorities believed were unlawful acts of Confederate guerrillas. In 1992, James McPherson argued that "the concept, and label, of total war" remained useful for describing the Civil War due to the extent and psychological impact of civilian property destruction. "The kind of conflict the Civil War had become merit[ed] the label of total war," even though the civilians were not directly targeted for killing. "From Limited to Total War," reprinted in *Drawn with the Sword: Reflections on the American Civil War*, 66, 70, 85 (1996). However, in a later review of Mark Grimsley's *The Hard Hand of War* (1995), Professor McPherson appears to have altered this view and accepted Grimsley's argument that the Confederate and Union armies tried to maintain fundamental distinctions between civilians and military personnel. "Hard war" and "directed severity" were more accurate descriptions of the Civil War than "total war." See "The

Hard Hand of War," reprinted in James M. McPherson, *This Mighty Scourge*, 123–29 (2007).

30. See Neely, *The Civil War and the Limits of Destruction*, 165–67.

31. Lincoln to Fell, December 20, 1859, *Collected Works*, vol. 3, 511.

32. Interview with Royal Clary, October (?) 1866, in *Herndon's Informants*, 370, 372 (Douglas L. Wilson and Rodney O. Davis 1998).

33. See ibid.; William G. Greene to William Herndon, May 30, 1865, and November 1, 1866, in *Herndon's Informants*, 17–18, 390 (Wilson and Davis).

34. See generally David Nichols, *Lincoln and the Indians*, 76–118 (1978); William Lee Miller, *President Lincoln: The Duty of a Statesman*, 322–26 (2008).

35. See William Dole to Caleb Smith, November 10, 1862, LOC Virtual Library.

36. Message to the Senate on Minnesota Indians, December 11, 1862, *Collected Works*, vol. 5, 550.

37. Thomas Goodrich, *Black Flag: Guerrilla Warfare on the Western Border 1861–1865*, 127–28 (1995).

38. William S. Rosecrans to Lincoln [with endorsement by Lincoln], March 12, 1864, LOC Virtual Library.

39. Lincoln to Rosecrans, April 4, 1864, *Collected Works*, vol. 7, 283–84.

40. David Herbert Donald, *Lincoln*, 489 (1995).

41. See generally Duane Schultz, *The Dahlgren Affair* (1998); Stephen W. Sears, "Raid on Richmond," in *Controversies and Commanders: Dispatches from the Army of the Potomac*, 225 (1999).

42. According to the 1863 annual report of General Ethan Allen Hitchcock, the U.S. officer in charge of prisoners exchanges, "an order was sent by the President to our commanders in the field not to grant paroles, and to make no exchanges, without orders from the War Department." Hitchcock to Stanton, November 30, 1863, in *Official Records*, series 2, vol. 6, 607–14.

43. See Kilpatrick to Parsons, February 16, 1864, *Official Records*, series 1, vol. 33, 172–73.

44. Proclamation of Amnesty and Reconstruction, December 8, 1863, *Collected Works*, vol. 7, 53.

45. See James M. McPherson, *Tried by War*, 207 (2008).

46. See Edwin C. Fishel, *The Secret War for the Union*, 256 (1996).

47. See Stephen W. Sears, *Gettysburg*, 354, 481 (2003).

48. Headquarters Army of the Potomac to Kilpatrick, February 27, 1864, *Official Records*, series 1, vol. 33, 173.

49. General Braxton Bragg to James Seddon, March 4, 1864, *Official Records*, series 1, vol. 33, 217.

50. Ibid., 219, 220.

51. See Sears, "Raid on Richmond," 245; "Colonel Ulric Dahlgren" (obituary), *Harper's Weekly*, March 26, 1864, 1.

52. Lee to Meade, April 15, 1864, *Official Records*, series 1, vol. 33, 178; Meade to Lee, April 17, 1864, *Official Records*, series 1, vol. 33, 180.

53. Quoted in Schultz, *The Dahlgren Affair*, 189.

54. An exception is Duane Schultz, who argues that the papers were Confederate fabrications intended to provide a justification in advance for covert operations against Northern cities, including use of biological agents and acts of arson. Ibid., 239–57.

55. Donald, *Lincoln*, 490.

56. See Fishel, *The Secret War for the Union*, 543.

57. See Sears, "Raid on Richmond," 233, 246–47.

58. See David E. Long, "A Time for Killing," in no. 1884 *Lincoln Lore*, 7 (Spring 2006); "Lincoln, Davis and the Dahlgren Raid," 9, no. 5 *North and South*, 70 (October 2006).

59. See Lincoln to Stanton, February 11, 1864, *Collected Works*, vol. 7, 179–80.

60. Lieber Code, article 50.

61. See Lieber Code, article 56, "A prisoner of war is subject to no punishment for being a public enemy, nor is any revenge wreaked upon him by the intentional infliction of any suffering, or disgrace, by cruel imprisonment, want of food, by mutilation, death, or any other barbarity," and article 59, "All prisoners of war are liable to the infliction of retaliatory measures."

62. Cartel for the Exchange of Prisoners of War between Great Britain and the United States of America, May 12, 1813, article 1, in *Documents on Prisoners of War*, 18–19 (U.S. Naval War College International Law Studies vol. 60, Howard Levie ed. 1979); The "Dix-Hill Cartel" for the General Exchange of Prisoners of War, entered into between the Union and Confederate Armies, article 1, in ibid., 34–36.

63. Lincoln to James C. Conkling, August 26, 1863, *Collected Works*, vol. 6, 406–7.

64. Ian Kershaw and Mark Seaman, *Operation Foxley: The British Plan to Kill Hitler*, 30 (1998).

65. Ibid., viii.

66. See Burrus M. Carnahan, *Act of Justice: Lincoln's Emancipation Proclamation and the Law of War*, 130 (2007).

67. Order of Retaliation, July 30, 1863, *Collected Works*, vol. 6, 357.

68. See, for example, the *Punch* cartoon described in Neely, *The Civil War and the Limits of Destruction*, 42–43 (2007).

69. See Sears, *Controversies and Commanders*, 242 (1999).

Conclusion

The chapter title quotation is from Lincoln to Stanton, Draft, March 18, 1864, *Collected Works*, vol. 7, 254, 255.

1. Lincoln to Stanton, Draft, March 18, 1864, *Collected Works*, vol. 7, 254, 255.

2. See Lieber Code, article 11, the law of war "disclaims all extortions and other transactions for individual gain; all acts of private revenge, or connivance at such acts"; article 16, "Military necessity does not admit of cruelty—that is, the infliction of suffering for the sake of suffering or for revenge"; article 28, "Retaliation will . . . never be resorted to as a measure of mere revenge, but only as a means of protective retribution"; article 56, "A prisoner of war is subject to no punishment for being a public enemy, nor is any revenge wreaked upon him by the intentional infliction of any suffering"; article 60, "It is against the usage of modern war to resolve, in hatred and revenge, to give no quarter"; article 68, "Unnecessary or revengeful destruction of life is not lawful."

3. Address before the Young Men's Lyceum of Springfield, Illinois, January 27, 1838, "The Perpetuation of Our Political Institutions," *Collected Works*, vol. 1, 108.

4. Allen Guelzo, "A. Lincoln, Philosopher," in *Lincoln's America, 1809–1865*, 7, 21 (Joseph Fornieri and Sarah Gabbard eds. 2008).

5. Lieber Code, article 14. In 1956, the U.S. Army refined the definition; military necessity was then declared to be a legal principle that justifies the use of measures "indispensable for securing the *complete* submission of the enemy *as soon as possible.*" Department of the Army Field Manual 27-10, *The Law of Land Warfare* (July 1956), para. 3 (emphasis added).

6. Lieber Code, article 15 (emphasis added).

7. Lincoln to Conkling, August 26, 1863, *Collected Works*, vol. 6, 406.

8. Message to Congress, March 6, 1862, *Collected Works*, vol. 5, 144, 145–46.

9. See Brady to Lincoln, February 15, 1865; Kennedy to Lincoln, March 14, 1865, LOC Virtual Library.

10. See General Order 24, Headquarters Department of the East, New York City, March 20, 1865, *Official Records*, series 2, vol. 8, 414; Nat Brandt, *The Man Who Tried to Burn New York* (1986); Duane Schultz, *The Dahlgren Affair*, 228–32 (1998).

11. Lincoln to Stanton, September 1, 1863, *Collected Works*, vol. 6, 427; Lincoln to Segar, September 5, 1863, and Note, *Collected Works*, vol. 6, 434.

12. See General Order 17, Headquarters Department of the East, New York City, February 21, 1865, *Official Records*, series 2, vol. 8, 279; Schultz, *The Dahlgren Affair*, 232–35.

13. See Browning to Lincoln, February 17, 1865; House of Representatives to Lincoln, February 17, 1865, LOC Virtual Library.

14. Stevens to Lincoln, February 24, 1865, LOC Virtual Library.

15. See Herndon's notes on interviews with John Todd Stuart and David Davis, in *Herndon's Informants*, 64, 350, 519 (Douglas L. Wilson and Rodney O. Davis 1998). It has been argued that belief in a universe obedient to a few natural laws was shared by Lincoln and his scientific contemporary Charles Darwin. See David R. Contosta, *Rebel Giants*, 62 (2008).

16. To Henry L. Pierce and Others, April 6, 1859, *Collected Works*, vol. 3, 374, 375.

17. See Mark E. Steiner, *An Honest Calling: The Law Practice of Abraham Lincoln*, 33–35 (2006).

18. Richard Carwardine, *Lincoln: A Life of Purpose and Power*, 259 (Knopf ed. 2006).

19. Quoted in Richard N. Current, *The Lincoln Nobody Knows*, 181 (1958; paperback ed. 1963). See also William Lee Miller's discussion of this quotation in *President Lincoln: The Duty of a Statesman*, 318–19 (2008).

20. Quoted in Allen Guelzo, "A. Lincoln, Philosopher," 22.

21. "Fragment on Niagara Falls," circa September 25–30, 1848, *Collected Works*, vol. 2, 10. See also Fred Kaplan, *Lincoln: Biography of a Writer*, 192–97 (2009).

22. Lincoln to Stanton, Draft, March 18, 1864, *Collected Works*, vol. 7, 254, 256.

23. Response to Serenade, November 10, 1864, *Collected Works*, vol. 8, 100, 101; see also Lincoln to Stanton, Draft, March 18, 1864, *Collected Works*, vol. 7, 254, 255.

24. For example, his letter to Secretary of State Seward of April 1, 1861, *Collected Works*, vol. 4, 316, and his letter to General Meade of July 14, 1863, *Collected Works*, vol. 6, 327.

25. Endorsement to John Hogan, February 13, 1864, *Collected Works*, vol. 7, 182–83.

26. Speech at Springfield, Illinois, June 26, 1857, *Collected Works*, vol. 2, 398, 400–401.

27. Lincoln to Bates, November 29, 1862, *Collected Works*, vol. 5, 515, 516.

28. Lincoln to Speed, July 4, 1842, *Collected Works*, vol. 1, 288, 289.

29. Lincoln to Hodges, April 4, 1864, *Collected Works*, vol. 7, 218, 282.

30. Herndon's notes on an interview with Mary Todd Lincoln, in *Herndon's Informants*, 358 (Wilson and Davis). Another set of notes on the interview substitutes "prayers" for "cares." Ibid., 360.

31. Swett to Herndon, January 17, 1866, in *Herndon's Informants*, 162 (Wilson and Davis).

32. See David Herbert Donald, *Lincoln*, 13–14 (1995).

33. See Allen Guelzo, *Redeemer President*, 325–27 (1999); Ronald White, *Lincoln's Greatest Speech: The Second Inaugural*, 135–41 (2002).

34. Lucas Morel, "Lincoln, God and Freedom: A Promise Fulfilled," in *Lincoln and Freedom: Slavery, Emancipation and the Thirteenth Amendment*, 48, 51 (2008).

35. *Collected Works*, vol. 5, 111.

36. Ibid., 115.

37. "He believed from the first, I think, that the agitation of Slavery would produce its overthrow. . . . His tactics were, to get himself in the right place and remain there still, until events would find him in that place." Swett to Herndon, January 17, 1866, in *Herndon's Informants*, 162 (Wilson and Davis). "I have no doubt that Mr. Lincoln believed that there was a predestined work for him in the world." Conversation with Hon. O. H. Browning at Leland Hotel Springfield June 17th 1875, in *An Oral History of Abraham Lincoln: John G. Nicolay's Interviews and Essays*, 1, 7 (Michael Burlingame ed. 1996).

38. Speech at Peoria, Illinois, October 16, 1854, *Collected Works*, vol. 2, 247, 255.

39. See Morel, "Lincoln, God and Freedom: A Promise Fulfilled," 48, 55–57.

40. "A House Divided," Speech at Springfield, Illinois, June 16, 1858, *Collected Works*, vol. 2, 461.

Index